CONTROLLING
THE
TONGUE

CONTROLLING
THE
TONGUE

R. T. KENDALL

Charisma
HOUSE
A STRANG COMPANY

Most Strang Communications/Charisma House/Siloam/FrontLine/Realms products are available at special quantity discounts for bulk purchase for sales promotions, premiums, fund-raising, and educational needs. For details, write Strang Communications/Charisma House/Siloam/FrontLine/ Realms, 600 Rinehart Road, Lake Mary, Florida 32746, or telephone (407) 333-0600.

CONTROLLING THE TONGUE by R. T. Kendall
Published by Charisma House: A Strang Company
600 Rinehart Road
Lake Mary, Florida 32746
www.charismahouse.com

Unless otherwise noted, all Scripture quotations are from the Holy Bible, New International Version. Copyright © 1973, 1978, 1984, International Bible Society. Used by permission.

Scripture quotations marked GNB are from *Good News Translation*, second edition. Copyright © 1992 by American Bible Society. Used by permission.

Scripture quotations marked JB are from *The Jerusalem Bible*, copyright © 1966, 1967, 1968 by Darton, Longman and Todd Ltd and Doubleday, a division of Random House, Inc.

Scripture quotations marked KJV are from the King James Version of the Bible.

Scripture quotations marked NEB are from *The New English Bible with the Apocrypha*, copyright © 1970 by Oxford University Press and Cambridge University Press.

Scripture quotations marked NKJV are from the New King James Version of the Bible. Copyright © 1979, 1980, 1982 by Thomas Nelson, Inc., publishers. Used by permission.

Scripture quotations marked NLT are from the Holy Bible, New Living Translation, copyright © 1996. Used by permission of Tyndale House Publishers, Inc., Wheaton, IL 60189. All rights reserved.

Scripture quotations marked PHILLIPS are from *The New Testament in Modern English*, revised edition. Copyright © 1958, 1960, 1972 by J. B. Phillips. Macmillan Publishing Co. Used by permission.

Scripture quotations marked TLB are from *The Living Bible*. Copyright © 1971. Used by permission of Tyndale House Publishers, Inc., Wheaton, IL 60189. All rights reserved.

Cover Designer, John Hamilton Design (www.johnhamiltondesign.com);
Design Director, Bill Johnson
Cover Illustration: Getty Images; Photographer: Jim Frazier

Library of Congress Cataloging-in-Publication Data
Kendall, R. T.
Controlling the tongue / by R. T. Kendall.
    p. cm.
Includes bibliographical references.
ISBN 978-1-59979-073-2 (hardback)
1. Oral communication--Religious aspects--Christianity. 2. Interpersonal communication-- Religious aspects--Christianity. I. Title.
BV4597.53.C64K46 2007
241'.672--dc22
                                    2006101015
This book was previously published as *Your Words Have Power* by Hodder and Stoughton, ISBN 978-0340-910177, copyright © 2006.
07 08 09 10 11 — 98765432
Printed in the United States of America

TO DALE

Contents

Foreword

I HAVE KNOWN RT FOR MORE THAN TWENTY years. He is an exceedingly close and treasured friend, and my understanding of Scripture and God's purpose for my own life has been immeasurably enriched by my close friendship with him.

One of the many things I admire about RT is that he is not ashamed to expose his greatest failures and weaknesses, to search for ways to overcome them, and then to seek to work it out daily in his own experience. He is a man who not only loves the truth but also longs with all his heart to "walk the talk" and then preach it!

This book is vintage RT, "warts 'n all." His sound biblical and practical remedies for the problems of the tongue are fantastic. For someone whose words in preaching and writing are his life's calling, it may surprise you to discover how much RT, like the rest of us, has also always struggled with the misuse of the tongue. I couldn't put the manuscript down, and as I read, I became aware afresh of a growing hunger and thirst for righteousness and holiness in my own heart and ever-increasing desire for purity in my thoughts and speech.

It seems an age since I have "heard" preaching like this, and so I wholeheartedly commend this book to you. By taking its principles to heart and calling on God's highest willingness to help us, each one of us can resolve to control our tongue and increasingly speak words that are edifying to others and glorifying to God.

I cannot thank God enough for what you are about to read. Prepare to be challenged, informed, convicted, enlightened, and shown the way of the Spirit—the pathway of love and self-control.

—LYNDON BOWRING

Preface

THERE IS A RATHER FUNNY STORY (IF A LITTLE complicated) that lies behind the making and the title of this book. When I was asked to list all my books at the end of *In Pursuit of His Glory* (Charisma House), the account of my twenty-five years at Westminster Chapel, I put my chosen title *Controlling the Tongue* for the second volume of my exposition of the Book of James, which at the time was not yet published. But when it emerged from the press, I noticed the British publisher called it *The Way of Wisdom.*

I gave it no more thought until Charisma House asked me to do my book *Controlling the Tongue*—which they picked out from the list in *In Pursuit of His Glory.* I pointed out that this book was an exposition of James 3–5 and was possibly not the sort of book they were expecting. So they asked, "Would you then do a book called *Controlling the Tongue*?" I agreed to this, and it is the book you now hold in your hands. However, my British publisher, for some reason, preferred the title *Your Words Have Power,* which is published in the UK.

I thank Jevon Bolden for her careful hand in editing the U.S. edition of this book. This is the first time she has been my editor, and I have been deeply impressed with her work. I also thank Barbara Dycus, Deborah Moss, and Ann Mulchan of Charisma

House and especially my friend Stephen Strang for the privilege of publishing this book.

I am grateful to my close friend Lyndon Bowring for writing the foreword. Lyndon, one of the most respected Christian leaders in Great Britain, is chairman of CARE in the UK, which has a close relationship with Focus on the Family in America. It was Lyndon, in fact, who introduced me to Dr. James Dobson—and our friendship took off from that moment.

This book is dedicated to my oldest friend—the Rev. W. Dale Martin. Dale is a retired minister of the Church of the Nazarene. Only eight days apart in our age, we grew up together in Ashland, Kentucky, graduated from the same high school, attended the same university, and have stayed in touch over the years. He and his lovely wife, Melba, live in Crossville, Tennessee.

Most of all, I thank my wife, Louise, my best friend and wisest critic, for her role in the making of this book. May God bless you as you read it.

—R. T. KENDALL
www.rtkendallministries.com

The wisdom that comes from heaven is first of all pure; then peace-loving, considerate, submissive, full of mercy and good fruit, impartial and sincere.

—JAMES 3:17

I DON'T WRITE ON THE SUBJECT OF CONTROLLING the tongue because I am an expert on it—or because I have mastered control of my own tongue. That would be like writing the book *Humility and How I Attained It*! Quite the contrary.

I write this because I have made nearly *every mistake imaginable* in this area. I have been in the ministry for over fifty years, and I am now seventy. When you reach my age, you take life, health, and death more seriously than in earlier years, and you think more and more about the remaining years and how it will be at the final judgment. I know one thing for sure: more than ever, I want to make every moment count, especially knowing that "we must all appear before the judgment seat of Christ, that each one may receive what is due him for the things done while in the body, whether good or bad" (2 Cor. 5:10). At that time God will "bring to light what is hidden in darkness and will expose the motives of men's hearts. At that time each will receive his praise from God" (1 Cor. 4:5).

Could I give you what is perhaps my most "unfavorite" verse in the Bible? It is Matthew 12:36—the words of Jesus: "I tell you that men will have to give account on the day of judgment for every careless word they have spoken." A careless word. "Idle word" (KJV). "Useless word" (GNB). "Thoughtless word" (NEB).

Oh, dear! I am in serious trouble. This does not make me look forward to the Day of Judgment.

I cannot think of anything scarier than having every careless word, idle word, useless word, or thoughtless word thrown up at me on that day. Imagine this: you are standing before the Lord with Him looking on, but also everybody else (this is further why it hurts so much). I don't know how it will happen—whether God gives earphones to everybody to eavesdrop on our conversations, in secret and public. I only know this is a word that I take seriously, and so should you. Were we to believe it literally, I can assure you that it would go a long way in helping us to control our tongues.

Consider the wisdom of these words: "Do not revile the king even in your thoughts, or curse the rich in your bedroom, because a bird of the air may carry your words, and a bird on the wing may report what you say" (Eccles. 10:20). As I hope there will be no wasted words in this book, I also hope that in my life—in public and in private, in the pulpit or with friends, with family or with strangers—I may make minimum unguarded comments that I will have to one day listen to before all people.

Two Definitions of Wisdom

Before we proceed further, we must define some terms, even if we think we already know what they mean. Controlling the tongue is self-restraint with words, having *the wisdom to know what to say*—and saying it—but equally knowing when *not* to speak—and saying nothing. Wisdom, or the lack of it, is what lies behind our conversations. This is why the apostle James, bringing to a conclusion his well-known discourse on the tongue said, "The *wisdom* that comes from heaven is first of all pure, then peace-loving, considerate, submissive, full of mercy and good fruit, impartial and sincere" (James 3:17, emphasis added).

General definition of wisdom

Wisdom may be defined two ways, both generally and particularly. The general definition embraces several words: *intelligence, insight, discernment, unusual knowledge and ability*—all of which are derived from the *fear of the Lord*. The first step toward finding true wisdom, therefore, is to fear the Lord: "The fear of the LORD is the beginning of wisdom" (Prov. 9:10). Wisdom is sometimes used interchangeably with understanding: "Wisdom is supreme; therefore get wisdom. Though it cost all you have [whatever else you get], get understanding" (Prov. 4:7). The word *understanding* in Hebraic thinking meant insight as a gift of God—not what one is born with or possesses naturally, but what the Lord bestows.

Like it or not, the only way to get true wisdom is to fear the Lord. A person may be born with a great intellect and not have wisdom. One may have great education and learning but not have wisdom. "Clever but not wise" is a phrase that may describe many a person with high profile in politics, education, government, business, finances, and also the ministry. The first step toward wisdom, therefore, is putting your relationship with God right, respecting Him and His Word, and making His honor your priority.

This is very important. If you and I are to benefit from a controlled tongue, we cannot bypass the most crucial and foundational principle of all: the fear of the Lord. Let no reader of this book delude himself or herself with the thought that you can pick up some "tips" on how to control the tongue by reading this book and at the same time ignore the fear of the Lord. This is not a secular book; it is not a "how to" book for people that are not interested in God or His Word. With deepest respect, you are a fool if you desire to learn how to control the tongue when there is not an underlying fear of God in your very being.

We never outgrow the fear of the Lord in the Christian life. It was the fear of the Lord that brought about our conversion in the first place. As the second verse of the famous hymn "Amazing Grace" puts it:

'Twas grace that taught my heart to fear,
And grace my fears relieved.
How precious did that grace appear,
The hour I first believed.[1]

—JOHN NEWTON

We must never think, for example, that we can outgrow asking God for mercy. We were initially converted by saying, "God, have mercy on me, a sinner"—or the equivalent words (Luke 18:13). Yet the most mature Christian still comes daily to the throne of grace to receive mercy (Heb. 4:16). So too with the fear of God; we must never, ever think we should outgrow the deepest respect and sense of awe toward God Almighty.

There is, however, a difference between the fear of God and the spirit of fear. God has not given us a spirit of fear or timidity or anxiety (2 Tim. 1:7). A spirit of fear leads to the opposite of tongue control. As a matter of fact, a spirit of fear produces what James calls *false wisdom*—that which is "earthly, unspiritual, of the devil" (James 3:15). A spirit of fear always leads to evil. (See Psalm 37:8.)

A spirit of fear is overcome by a true fear of God—a care to please Him in all our ways. This care to please Him is what leads to wisdom. You will not even come close to controlling the tongue if you dismiss these lines. Only the fear of the Lord leads to true wisdom. Wisdom, therefore, is the key to self-control. One of the fruit of the Spirit is self-control (Gal. 5:23). This, then, is what I mean by a general definition of *wisdom*.

Particular definition of wisdom

A particular definition of *wisdom* is knowing what to do next and having the ability to carry it out. Particular wisdom, therefore, is knowing what is the next step forward. We all should pray for this kind of wisdom every day, just as we should pray every day for the ability to control the tongue and have self-restraint with words. Wisdom with the tongue is knowing what to *say* next—and saying it; and having the self-discipline *not to speak* when you have the presence of mind that keeping your mouth shut truly is the next step forward. Controlling the tongue is having the wisdom to know what to say and what not to say, saying what is wise and not speaking at all when this is wise.

James puts our minds at ease when he says that if we are never at fault in what we say, we are *perfect* (James 3:2). But none of us are perfect! As the New Living Translation puts it, "Those who control their tongues can also control themselves in every other way." Tongue control is a noble goal; it leads to self-discipline in every area of our lives.

We will never be perfect in this life. This is because we have our fallen nature with us always. "The heart is deceitful above all things and beyond cure. Who can understand it?" (Jer. 17:9). What we inherited from our first parents in the Garden of Eden we will have until we are glorified, when we are totally changed (1 Cor. 15:51). Until then we are conscious of indwelling sin, the propensity to impure thoughts, unguarded comments, imperfections that keep embarrassing us, and weaknesses that reveal we have not been glorified yet. Until then, we will err.

But this does not mean we should not try to be and do better! This is one of the big differences between the Christian and the non-Christian: it is being a Christian that makes one want to get it right. We have a motivation to be more like Jesus. We want to please God more and more. We want a greater testimony before others—saved and lost. Because we *can indeed improve*! I think of John Newton's words to his friend William Cowper, when they were discussing Paul's words, "But by the grace of God I am what I am, and his grace to me was not without effect" (1 Cor. 15:10). Newton looked across the breakfast table at Cowper and said:

> I am not what I ought to be.... Not what I wish to be....
> I am not what I hope to be.... Not what I once was.... "By the
> grace of God I am what I am."[2]

The ultimate proof of words spoken in wisdom is Scripture itself. Our doctrine of the inspiration of the Bible comes into focus here. I believe in the infallibility of Holy Scripture, that it is totally inspired by the Holy Spirit—from Genesis to Revelation. This is because "all Scripture is God-breathed and is useful for teaching, rebuking, correcting and training in righteousness, so that the man of God may be thoroughly equipped for every good work" (2 Tim. 3:16–17). The origin of Scripture is not in man, but "men spoke from God as they were carried along by the Holy Spirit" (2 Pet. 1:21).

I write this book to encourage you. You will see you are not alone in losing control with the tongue. We all have this problem. I also write this book to challenge you. One of the greatest challenges we face is to master the tongue. I do believe this book can make a difference in your own life. That is the main purpose in writing it. I pray this book will mark a turning point in your pilgrimage—that it will lead to your receiving a reward at the judgment seat of Christ. As we will see more clearly later, what Jesus said in Matthew 12:36 is not a reference to whether you are saved or lost, but whether you receive a reward as a Christian on that day.

I blush to think of the words I have uttered, the gossip I have listened to and helped spread, the things I have said in order to discredit my enemies, the language I have used when I lost my temper, and not to mention what people remember— whether or not there may be some plausible explanation for my ill-chosen utterances. Once we've said it, whether in public, in private, or in print—it is *done*. People don't forget.

The Moving Finger writes; and, having writ,

Moves on: nor all your Piety nor Wit

Shall lure it back to cancel half a Line,

Nor all your Tears wash out a Word of it.[3]

—OMAR KHAYYAM (1048–1122)

PART ONE

FAILURE IN CONTROLLING THE TONGUE

*Now these things occurred as examples to keep us from setting
our hearts on evil things as they did.*

—1 CORINTHIANS 10:6

ONE WAY OF UNDERSTANDING CONTROLLING
the tongue is by seeing examples of what self-restraint with
words most certainly is not. We will do this in this section by
examining biblical examples—when people in the Old and New
Testaments failed to show wisdom and, in the following section,
when they got it right.

The infallible Word of God describes fallible men and
women between its covers. What Scripture says about them we
can believe, but what some of them *did* and what they *said* at
times were very often wrong. So even the best of God's servants
described in the Bible frequently turn out to be examples of how
not to be! Never forget that God records the bad that they did
"as examples to keep us from setting our hearts on evil things as
they did" (1 Cor. 10:6). In other words, we don't need to repeat
the same mistakes!

I have lived long enough to observe that sooner or later every person I begin to admire a little bit too much disappoints me. We may wish that we had lived in Bible times to witness firsthand some of the great people in biblical history—Abraham, Isaac, Jacob, David, or Elijah, for example—and find out what they were really like, but you would have been shocked to see how human they were. They were not perfect. The imperfection was almost always traceable to the tongue.

What we say reveals the heart: "Out of the overflow of the heart the mouth speaks" (Matt. 12:34). This is why Jesus said by our *words* we are either "acquitted" or "condemned" (v. 37) when the verdict is given as to our reward at the judgment seat of Christ. Our words, which reveal to what extent we truly sought after true wisdom, therefore indicate what was in the heart.

We now turn to some biblical examples of *how not to be*. We will examine various categories of verbal sin and see people, some of them among God's best, who failed in the matter of controlling the tongue. We will do this by observing typical sins we have all committed, at least to some degree. They reveal various weaknesses and typical failures in controlling the tongue. All these have their origin in our fallen nature.

Chapter One

POINTING THE FINGER

You, therefore, have no excuse, you who pass judgment on someone else, for at whatever point you judge the other, you are condemning yourself, because you who pass judgment do the same things.

—ROMANS 2:1

THE PROPHET ISAIAH PROMISED ANCIENT ISRAEL that the breakthrough they were hoping for—namely, that God would show up—would never come until certain conditions were met. Among these conditions was doing away with "the yoke of oppression, with the pointing finger and malicious talk" (Isa. 58:9). When people are constantly blaming each other, no breakthrough will likely come. Many marriages could be saved overnight if both husband and wife would stop pointing the finger.

Blaming one another is a very natural practice. It is certainly not the working of the Holy Spirit. It springs from nature. It takes no education or training on "how to learn to point the finger." This practice comes straight out of the Garden of Eden immediately after our first parents sinned. They started it, and all of us have been doing it ever since.

1. Adam, blaming God and his wife, Eve, immediately after his sin in the Garden of Eden

The first conversation God had with Adam after the Fall in the Garden of Eden finds Adam blaming not himself but his wife, Eve, for his partaking of the forbidden fruit. But if you look closely at these words, you will see that Adam was actually pointing the finger at God Himself: "The woman *you* put here with me—she gave me some fruit from the tree, and I ate it" (Gen. 3:12, emphasis added). This was a dead giveaway that depravity had set in Adam's heart. Corruption and vileness of the human heart have been with every man, every woman, and every child—of all races, cultures, and colors—ever since. Instinctively we do not see our own sin but that of others. We want to blame God, then others—but never ourselves if we can help it.

One of the irrefutable proofs that we are sinners is that we want to defend ourselves, shift the blame to someone else, and avoid as long as possible the matter of admitting to our guilt. Essential to our natural depravity is self-righteousness. We were born with it. We did not need to attend Harvard or Oxford to learn how to be self-righteous. It is the most natural inclination in the world! It is intrinsic to our nature.

Adam revealed that sin had set in already when God came looking for him in the Garden of Eden, asking, "Where are you?" (Gen. 3:9). Adam did not want to face God and own his own guilt. Trying to shift the blame when it is our own fault is evidence of our sin of self-righteousness. Pointing the finger also shows we have lost control of the tongue.

We all have these evil thoughts. No matter how mature we become in the Christian faith, evil thoughts will emerge in our hearts. Why? Because we are imperfect. I say it again, we will not be perfect until we are glorified and are changed to be like Jesus. (See 1 John 3:3; Romans 8:30.) In the meantime, vile thoughts enter our minds, and we instinctively want to lash out at God or at others, "Why did you do this to me? Why did you let this happen?"

Controlling the tongue is having the wisdom not to say everything that enters our minds, including what we say to God. Yes, God knows we have these thoughts. He knows, too, when *we refuse to say* what enters our brains. He applauds us when we show wisdom.

You may say, "But if you have the thought, you might as well say it since God knows what you are thinking." Wrong. Don't *say* it. Wisdom is self-control, not the least being when you talk to God. "By your *words* [not what you may momentarily *think*] you will be condemned" (Matt. 12:37, emphasis added). It is what we *say* that gets us into trouble. Here is a prayer you and I cannot pray too often:

> May the words of my mouth and the meditation of my heart
> be pleasing in your sight,
> O LORD, my Rock and my Redeemer.
>
> —PSALM 19:14

Or think about these words:

Do not be quick with your mouth,
　do not be hasty in your heart
　to utter anything before God.
God is in heaven
　and you are on earth,
　so let your words be few.

—ECCLESIASTES 5:2

2. Jacob, verbally abusing his own children

Jacob was the expert in pointing the finger. He loved to blame others, especially his sons. He did this with Simeon and Levi. Instead of giving them credit for wanting to preserve the honor of his daughter, Dinah, he only thought of how he would appear to others: "You have brought trouble on me by making me a stench to the Canaanites and Perizzites, the people living in this land" (Gen. 34:30).

Jacob even blamed his sons for the fact that the prime minister of Egypt demanded to see Benjamin: "Why did you bring this trouble on me by telling the man you had another brother?" (Gen. 43:6).

Jacob is arguably the worst parent that ever lived. He showed favoritism by giving undue attention to Joseph and blamed the other sons for his own sense of guilt. He was an expert in making them feel guilty. It is like my friend J. John, the great British evangelist, said, "My mother was a travel agent; she sends people on guilt trips." Jacob did that all the time.

It is our *words* that make the difference. It is what our children *hear* that affects them. We may have thoughts—which may or may not be true—but when we utter them the damage is done.

In my book *In Pursuit of His Glory*, an account of my twenty-five years as minister of Westminster Chapel, London, I close with a section "If I Could Turn the Clock Back"—and refer to how I would have put my family first, not my ministry, had I those years to live over again.[1] But I could add volumes to that. I feel I have made almost every mistake that can be made when it comes to sending our children on guilt trips. I am too much like Jacob.

I don't want this book to send you on a guilt trip. We have all failed. These lines are from a mature minister of God who is trying to pass on a bit of wisdom to the next generation. Don't feel guilty. Read on; I will deal with guilt over regrettable words before the end of this book. But if there are those who read this who can put things right by ceasing to blame people—their children, their spouse, their friends, those around them—this book will be worth its weight in gold.

3. Sarah, blaming Abraham for Hagar and Ishmael

"You are responsible for the wrong I am suffering" (Gen. 16:5). But it was Sarah's own suggestion that he sleep with Hagar—her maidservant—in order that Sarah could "build a family through her" (v. 2). The result of this union was that Hagar gave birth to Ishmael. This caused immense problems in the household.

Once we realize we made a wrong decision, our self-righteous nature often lures us into thinking it was not our fault—but someone else's. So we blame others. We do this because we feel so guilty ourselves. Those who carry the greatest sense of guilt are brilliant in giving guilt trips. Or to put it the other way around, those who give the greatest guilt trips usually have the deepest sense of guilt themselves. We foolishly think that pointing the finger is going to shift the blame and make us feel better.

Many marriages can be healed overnight if both the husband and the wife would *stop pointing the finger*. It is our words that make the other feel bad. If we would stop keeping a record of wrongs in our marriage, we would be miles ahead. Love "keeps no record of wrongs" (1 Cor. 13:5). Why do we keep records? To prove that we paid, to prove we said this, promised that. But love will tear the records up—so they cannot be referred to again. But when we *keep* the record of the wrong, it is because in that moment we have already decided to refer to it one day. "I will remember that. I won't forget that," the husband says to the wife. And he keeps his word. The marriage could be on the rocks.

Abraham and Sarah survived. But her pointing the finger put a severe strain on their marriage. It shows that the best of God's servants have marriage and family problems. But so many of them could be avoided if we stopped playing the blame game.

Adam, Jacob, and Sarah were just as guilty of wrongdoing as the people they blamed. Just as God expresses forgiveness toward us, we too can put things right in our relationships by ceasing to blame others and forgive.

In this next chapter we will explore how self-pity does not move the heart of God to rescue us, but to many of us it just feels right. We will look at many of God's own servants who fell prey to it.

Chapter Two

SELF-PITY

Everything is against me!

—GENESIS 42:36

SELF-PITY IS FEELING SORRY FOR YOURSELF. YOU feel that you are the object of unfair treatment, that you have had to carry a load that few, if any, understand or appreciate. You perhaps feel you were unlucky with having the parents you had, the environment you grew up in, the education you received. You may have been abused by an authority figure, lied about, rejected, and discriminated against. Whenever you get a chance to excel, something happens to derail what had possibilities. The future looks bleak, life is passing you by, and there is little to live for.

President John F. Kennedy used to say, "Life's not fair." I do not know what made him say that. He had far more advantages than most, but perhaps he was thinking of less fortunate people than himself. Whatever, what he said is true. It is a wicked world.

Some think that being a Christian will eliminate all that is not good. But bad things happen to God's best, and often good things happen to the vile and venal. A Christian soon discovers that God allows injustice to happen to him or her, and such a person is then challenged whether to complain or accept adversity with dignity.

Self-pity is not acceptable for the Christian, although we all have been guilty of this. If anything, I feel I have at times been the world's worst. Self-pity always feels right at the time, but it is almost always counterproductive when you vocalize it. Feel it if you must, but verbalizing those feelings does not move the heart of God to come to your rescue. He is more likely to wait a while and lead you step by step to grow up so that one day you can help others who have the same problem.

We now look at some classic examples of God's most famous servants who fell prey to self-pity. It may be somewhat consoling that you are in good company!

1. Jacob, refusing to be comforted after believing that Joseph was dead

Yes, Jacob heads the list again. Isn't it comforting to know that even God's chief instruments made so many horrendous mistakes? I find this consoling, especially since I identify with Jacob so much!

One day Jacob's sons sold their brother Joseph to the Ishmaelites. Rather than tell Jacob what they did, they took Joseph's coat of many colors and dipped it in blood—then laid it before Jacob. He took the bait, asserting that Joseph was devoured by a wild animal. All his sons tried to comfort him, "but he refused to be comforted. 'No,' he said, 'in mourning I will go down to the grave'" (Gen. 37:35).

Self-pity is a sin against God. Jacob should have known better. True, the evidence was convincing. But the promises God gave to him, as well as those concerning his twelve sons—their posterity and prosperity—should have held him. He gave in to unbelief. God heard his words. The angels must have blushed. When we utter words of self-pity, it exposes our unbelief and lack of confidence in God, not to mention that it is a poor testimony. For as Romans 14:23 says, "Everything that does not come from faith is sin."

2. Jacob, bearing a negative testimony to Pharaoh

Jacob exhibited self-pity again when he was introduced to Pharaoh years later. He had so much to praise God for. Joseph was alive! He was second only to Pharaoh in Egypt. All Jacob's children and grandchildren were preserved in the famine. All that God promised him through dreams and visions was coming to pass. What goodness and mercy had been extended to Jacob.

And now Jacob had an opportunity to witness to the greatest king in the world. This was his moment. It does not come around to many people. What do you suppose Jacob said to Pharaoh? He said, "My years have been few and difficult, and they do not equal the years of the pilgrimage of my fathers" (Gen. 47:9). Never mind that Jacob was one hundred thirty years old! Here he was in Egypt and restored to Joseph (who was alive and well and the prime minister), but still complaining. It was not the best testimony before Pharaoh. He had every reason to rejoice. But no. He still complained.

How many of us would like to see a videotape of our words played to the world when we had every reason under the sun to be thankful but complained instead?

3. Elijah, claiming before God and men that he was the only prophet alive

Speaking to none other than God, Elijah said, "I have been very zealous for the LORD God Almighty. . . . I am the only one left, and now they are trying to kill me too" (1 Kings 19:14). First of all, Elijah was not the only prophet left and should have known better. Obadiah had taken a hundred prophets and hid them in a cave—and Elijah knew that (1 Kings 18:1–15). There were a good number of prophets around. But owing to persecution, Elijah was feeling sorry for himself. He took himself too seriously.

Self-pity often masks a feeling of self-importance, and both spring from self-righteousness. Once before, Elijah had stated publicly that he was the only prophet left—and uttered these thoughtless words before hundreds of the prophets of Baal. "I am the only one of the LORD's prophets left," he proclaimed (1 Kings 18:22). It shows he had completely dismissed those one hundred prophets that Obadiah preserved. He thought he was a cut above them, that he was the only true prophet.

God is so patient with us when we utter foolish comments like that. Had God required sinless perfection before Elijah could be used, God would have interrupted the proceedings at Mount Carmel at once and called the whole thing off. God could have thundered, "No, you are quite wrong," and stopped the whole thing. But He let Elijah continue.

It was some time later that God said, as it were, "Oh, by the way, Elijah, you might like to know that I have reserved *seven thousand* who have not bowed down to Baal." (See 1 Kings 19:18.) God patiently waited for the right time to deal with Elijah.

So too with us. When I think of my own self-importance and self-pity over the years—when I had so much to be thankful for and no right to be used—I blush that God continued to use me.

4. *Job and Jeremiah, cursing the day of their births*

We can sympathize with their plight. There is Job, not understanding what was going on when he lost everything, including his good health, and Jeremiah, being accused of treason because of his prophecies that Babylon would destroy Jerusalem.

There is often a reasonable explanation for a person giving in to self-pity. What Job suffered was extremely hard. But openly cursing the day of one's birth did not bless the Creator and was a terrible thing to utter (Job 3:1ff). He asked, "Why did I not perish at birth, and die as I came from the womb?" (Job 3:11). As for the prophet Jeremiah, he said, "Cursed be the day I was born!" (Jer. 20:14). Imagine a sovereign vessel who speaks for God talking like that!

The Holy Spirit did not lead either Jeremiah or Job to speak in this manner. The Holy Spirit, however, preserved their words for us to read. This is what they actually said, but that does not make it right merely because we know all ended well. We are not given these examples for us to imitate. We are given them, at least partly, for us to see that the best of God's children get extremely discouraged and say regrettable things.

5. Jonah, when his prophecy to Nineveh was not vindicated

God told Jonah to go to Nineveh and prophesy against it (Jon. 1:2). He disobeyed and sought refuge in a ship sailing to Tarshish (Spain). But on the journey God sent such a storm that the sailors (at Jonah's request) threw him overboard, and Jonah was swallowed up by a great fish. While in the belly of the fish, Jonah repented and prayed that God might be gracious and let him do the very thing he had rebelled against. God was gracious and gave Jonah a second chance, telling him to go to Nineveh (Jon. 3:1). He did, proclaiming, "Forty more days and Nineveh will be overturned" (v. 4).

What Jonah feared most is exactly what happened. The people of Nineveh believed this word and repented—from the king down to the least person. Instead of destroying Nineveh, which Jonah was on record for promising, God showed mercy on them and "did not bring upon them the destruction he had threatened" (v. 10).

Most preachers would have been thrilled from head to toe to see God move like that. But not Jonah. He was more interested in his prophecy being fulfilled—so he would be vindicated as a prophet—than he was in seeing the people of Nineveh spared.

Therefore, instead of rejoicing in a saved nation, "Jonah was greatly displeased and became angry" (Jon. 4:1). It is surprising to many that a true man of God could have such a big ego and be so selfish. But Jonah 4:1–11 is an account of a person being overcome by self-pity: "Now, O LORD, take away my life, for it is better for me to die than to live" (v. 3). In other words, Jonah would rather die than have the people of Nineveh live; he preferred their death to his embarrassment!

What is most extraordinary is the endless patience God had with Jonah. We might expect God to judge Jonah on the spot, but instead the Lord gently dealt with Jonah and brought him to a place of repentance. "Have you any right to be angry?" God asked Jonah (v. 4).

Our vocalizing self-pity, even when we are telling it to God, can bring us to such a distorted sense of right and wrong that we give God an invitation to judge us. He could do that. But just as He was patient with Jonah, I know He has been patient with me. I identify with Jonah—all the way from his initial disobedience to his inexcusable self-pity. I have been Jonah more often than I want you to know. I would hate for you to eavesdrop on my words when my pride was threatened. You would be shocked. But God was patient with me, just as He was with Jonah.

How do we know Jonah repented? Because, in telling the whole story of what happened, he gave God the last word (Jon. 4:10–11). When our words come back to haunt us and show how low we can stoop in needing our self-esteem bolstered, we must thank God for His gracious dealings with us—and then stop arguing with Him. Give Him the last word.

Chapter Three

MANIPULATING PROVIDENCE

There is no wisdom, no insight, no plan that can succeed against the LORD.

—PROVERBS 21:30

GOD'S PROVIDENCE IS HIS OVERRULING WILL in all our affairs. He makes things happen. It is important to remember this: *God has a plan*—a will of His own. He has already decided what is good and right and what is best for us; He works all things after the counsel of His own will (Eph. 1:11). Only a fool will try to upstage what God has already determined. But sometimes the best of God's people do foolish things.

This often happens when we think He is not working fast enough or that He has forgotten us or even that He did not mean what He said! We tend to think sometimes that we can step into His affairs and give Him a little help! The truth is, He doesn't want our help, and He certainly doesn't like it one bit if we think we have more wisdom than He has.

1. Joseph, when he tried to vindicate himself

After being falsely accused by Potiphar's wife (she accused him of trying to rape her), Joseph was put in prison. He was understandably angry and displeased. He had been betrayed by his brothers, and now this! He was a frustrated man. So when he saw a chance to get out of prison, he seized it. Prophesying to the king's cupbearer that he would get his job back in three days, Joseph inserted himself into the picture, like this: "Remember me and show me kindness; mention me to Pharaoh and get me out of this prison.... I have done nothing to deserve being put in a dungeon" (Gen. 40:14–15). One truly sympathizes with Joseph.

But God wasn't having it! God had big plans for him. Had God permitted the cupbearer to deliver this message to Pharaoh before the right time, Joseph would have forfeited a brilliant future. Fortunately, the cupbearer forgot to mention this to Pharaoh. I personally think that God looked down into Joseph's cell and said, "Oh, Joseph, you should not have said that to the cupbearer. I think you will need a couple more years there."

Love is not "self-seeking" (1 Cor. 13:5). Had Joseph been utterly devoid of bitterness, he would not have promoted himself like that. Had he already *totally* forgiven his brothers (and all others who hurt him) for what they did, I believe he would have been so filled with the Spirit of God that he would have known it was wrong to speak like that to the cupbearer. God wanted to promote Joseph without Joseph's manipulation. He wanted to show Joseph and Israel what can be done without any human help!

We all are tempted to nudge the arm of providence. We want to pull strings to get to the next level. Perhaps God permits this at times. But for the *big things* He has in mind for us, I myself have learned to let God do this! I would be afraid to promote myself lest I promote myself to the level of my incompetence! When we totally let God take charge, we will learn that He wants to do things for us in such a manner that we will always know it is what God did—and not us!

2. The Israelites, claiming they could still enter Canaan when God swore that they couldn't

God sent twelve spies into the Promised Land to investigate the situation. Ten out of the twelve came back convinced that the Israelites dare not proceed into the land God had given Israel as an inheritance. "We can't attack those people; they are stronger than we are," said the ten spies. "We seemed like grasshoppers in our own eyes, and we looked the same to them" (Num. 13:31, 33).

Caleb and Joshua, however, said in so many words, "We can do it—let's go for it" (v. 30). They were not given into unbelief like the majority.

But the majority ruled. It certainly was not the "sanctified majority." It was the unbelieving majority. The next night the people grumbled against Moses and wished they had died in Egypt. The whole assembly talked about stoning Joshua and

Caleb. This is when God made a proposition with Moses to destroy the people and start all over again and Moses interceded on their behalf. Although God heard Moses' prayer—"I have forgiven them, as you asked"—He nonetheless vowed that "not one of the men who saw my glory and the miraculous signs I performed...will ever see the land" (Num. 14:20–23). This is when God swore in His wrath that they would not enter into His rest. (See Hebrews 3:11.)

When God swears, it is "all over"—period. There are no further conditions or qualifications—as in a general promise. A promise is usually given on a condition. But if God *swears*, there is nothing more that we can do. We cannot persuade Him otherwise, no matter how many promises we make, no matter how hard we try. If He swears, that's it.

That is what happened with ancient Israel. God swore in His wrath that the people would not be allowed into Canaan—at all. And Moses told them that. And then, would you believe it, the people repented and said, "We have sinned...we will go up..." (Num. 14:40). Speaking like this is challenging God's wisdom and trying to overrule His providence, so Moses warned them, "Do not go up, because the LORD is not with you. You will be defeated by your enemies" (v. 42). But they ignored Moses's warning, went toward the hill country, and utterly failed (Num. 14:44–45).

Our words cannot change God's mind when He has uttered an oath. There are these two unchangeable things—the promise and the oath. (See Hebrews 6:17–18.) As long as there is a promise extended to us, we should take it with both hands. But when God declares His word in an oath, nothing will change His mind, no matter how long we talk or how loud we cry.

3. Absalom, promoting himself to the kingship

After King David's sin (page 47), the beginnings of Nathan's prophecy that "the sword will never depart from your house" (2 Sam. 12:10) began to emerge. Probably the greatest grief David would suffer was from his own son Absalom. Absalom was angry with his father for refusing to see his face after he took vengeance upon his brother Amnon for raping his sister. (See 2 Samuel 13; 14:24.) He did something that eventually resulted in his forcing his father, King David, into exile.

Whereas God did not let Joseph's nudging the arm of providence succeed, He did allow Absalom to get his way—for a while.

Here is the way it started. Absalom provided himself with a chariot and horses and with fifty men to run ahead of him. He took a position near the city gate where everyone saw him. When people had their complaints to be placed before the king, Absalom would do things to endear himself to the people so they would be diverted from seeing the king. He flattered the people who came along and in an evil manner began to undermine the king with poisonous words.

Here was a typical conversation. Once he found out where a person was from, Absalom would say, "Look, your claims are valid and proper, but there is no representative of the king to hear you." He would add, "If only I were appointed judge in the land! Then everyone who had a complaint or case could come to me and I would see that he gets justice" (2 Sam. 15:3–4). Therefore when people came into the city, he would reach out his hand and kiss the person, bowing. "Absalom behaved in this way toward all the Israelites who came to the king asking for justice, and so *he stole the hearts* of the men of Israel" (v. 6, emphasis added).

There have been not a few number-two men in various churches who have done this sort of thing. Not content to be number two, to which they had been called, they would undermine the leadership of the senior minister by flattering the people, making the true leader look detached from everybody and winning the hearts of the flock before the people realized what was happening. This is why every leader needs *loyalty* almost above anything else when looking for people to join the staff.

God had put David in the kingship. But David had sinned, and his kingdom was beginning to fall apart in places, not the least of which was in his own family.

Absalom succeeded. He tricked his father, David, into thinking he was going to worship the Lord in Hebron. Instead Absalom had arranged people to shout, "Absalom is king in Hebron," when the trumpets sounded. The report came to King David, saying, "The hearts of the men of Israel are with Absalom" (2 Sam. 15:13). The result was David being forced into exile. It was one of the saddest moments in his life.

David was eventually restored, and Absalom was tragically killed, literally being hung by his own hair (2 Sam. 18:9–10). Even sadder, if this were possible, was the fact that Absalom built a monument to himself. He had erected it during his lifetime, thinking, "I have no son to carry on the memory of my name." So he named the pillar after himself (2 Sam. 18:18).

People who usurp the providence of God to advance themselves are doomed from the start. Although it would not have happened had David not sinned as he did, God still will punish those who foolishly promote themselves. The most they get is a monument to themselves, a stone that but reminds future generations of their utter folly.

Absalom's folly began with the tongue. He appeared to succeed for a while. He won the battle but lost the war.

Chapter Four

TRYING TO PROVE OURSELVES

You are the ones who justify yourselves in the eyes of men, but God knows your hearts. What is highly valued among men is detestable in God's sight.

—LUKE 16:15

M Y OLD FRIEND PETE CANTRELL OFTEN SAYS, "The greatest freedom is having nothing to prove." I think this is one of the profoundest words I have ever heard. The person who needs to prove how right or how strong he or she is, is one who is not free. There is a struggle inside to make others think they are right and strong. The truth is, if we really are right and strong, we don't have to say anything! Freedom is being experienced, therefore, when one has nothing to prove. He or she does not need to justify himself or herself; neither do they need to make themselves look good. For people like that, it is enough that *God knows*. (See John 5:44.)

1. Job, when he broke silence with his "friends"

After Job lost his wealth and health, his three friends joined him. They came to comfort him. At first they saw him from a distance. They could hardly recognize him and began to weep openly. They tore their robes and sprinkled dust on their heads. They sat on the ground with him for seven days and nights: "*No one said a word* to him, because they saw how great his suffering was" (Job 2:13, emphasis added).

Who broke the silence? It was Job. This was a mistake. He was not required to say a word. If they were truly his friends, let *them* speak! But Job spoke first. He almost certainly knew what they were thinking—knowing traditional theology about sin and suffering. They thought that Job had sin in his life or this would not have happened. He felt a need to say something. He was not aware of a conscious sin against God, but he knew what they were thinking in their hearts, so he wanted to say something that would at least imply how innocent he was. This was the first mistake—speaking at all. As my friend Pete Cantrell says, which I referred to at the beginning of this chapter, the greatest freedom is having nothing to prove. But Job felt a need to break the silence.

The most natural feeling in the world is the urge to have your name cleared from blame. I know what it is to want vindication more than anything. One of the greatest lessons I have had to learn in fifty years of ministry is, *let God do it*. Everything God does is better than what any of us could do. But if there is *anything* that God does best (if I may put it that way), it is the job of vindicating. He does it so brilliantly. If *we* interfere, He backs off. We therefore never know what might have been had He been free to do His job. When it comes to vindicating, He makes it clear that it is His sole prerogative: "It is mine to avenge; I will repay" (Rom. 12:19).

2. Rehoboam, when he boasted of personal strength

The son of Solomon was implored to make the people's burdens lighter. He said he would think about it. When he sought the advice of some his lifelong friends from his youth, they told him to say some of the saddest words in Holy Writ. I cringe every time I read this: "My little finger is thicker than my father's waist. My father laid on you a heavy yoke; I will make it even heavier" (1 Kings 12:10–11). Sadly, Rehoboam did just as they said.

It is small men who talk like this. They have a need to prove themselves and show how strong, how manly, how secure they are. Rehoboam's decision was a turning point in the ancient history of Israel. He was afraid of being seen as less than strong. He knew how highly respected his father was. He thought he would get more respect by showing what a tyrant is like. He lost—everybody lost.

Paul said that Jesus was crucified in "weakness" (2 Cor. 13:4), which in fact showed our Lord's greatest strength. He had the power to call ten thousand angels to come down and deliver Him. He who raised the dead and walked on water could have come down from the cross the moment He was challenged to do so. But no. He let them do what they did. He lost the battle in order to win the war—our redemption.

When we have a need to show how strong we are, I think of Shakespeare's famous line, "The lady protests too much, methinks."[1] The greatest strength is having the confidence to prove nothing at the time in order that God will show His glory and power in His time.

3. The Pharisee in the temple, trying to justify himself

Jesus gave one of His best-known parables, describing a tax collector and a Pharisee. The Pharisee said, "God, I thank you that I am not like other men—robbers, evildoers, adulterers—or even like this tax collector. I fast twice a week and give a tenth of all I get" (Luke 18:10–12). Jesus gave this parable to those who were "confident of their own righteousness" (v. 9). The funny thing is, they needed to prove themselves, like the Pharisee—"I am not like others." Shakespeare said, "Comparisons are odorous,"[2] but the worst kind of doing that is when you think you are a cut above others. And when you have a need to say something that makes yourself look good in the light of a person who seems so bad by comparison, it is because you are not free—and in the case of the Pharisee, not justified before God.

It was the tax collector, however, who would not even look up to heaven but beat his breast and said, "God, have mercy on me, a sinner" (v. 13). According to Jesus, it was the tax collector, not the Pharisee, who was justified before God (v. 14).

When you are justified before God, you are free. Seeking to be justified, or vindicated, before people is a crippling, endless, and counterproductive enterprise; you are never at peace. You have no freedom. But when you know that *God Himself* declares you righteous, you are free and have no need to get your satisfaction from comparing yourself with others.

The heart of the gospel is at stake here. What justifies us before God—our good works? Or is it our confession to God that we are sinners? Answer: we are justified when we do not try to prove ourselves before God but lean on His mercy. A person is converted by asking God for mercy. Not only that, but in this very parable the Greek behind the word *mercy* really means, "God, be propitiated for me." The Greek word is *hilaskomai,* a word that corresponds to "mercy seat," the place in the holy of holies where the blood made atonement for sins. Jesus used a word that combined not only mercy but also the need for the sacrifice of blood. This is what the tax collector was pleading in his behalf—not his works.

When we trust our works, there will always be a need to try to prove ourselves—by words. The greatest freedom is having nothing to prove. This freedom comes when we put all our "eggs into one basket," namely, the death of Jesus on the cross. That brings freedom because this alone is what justifies us before God.

Chapter Five

SPEAKING OUT OF FEAR

Do not be anxious about anything.

—PHILIPPIANS 4:6

SPEAKING OUT OF FEAR ALWAYS LEADS TO EVIL (Ps. 37:8). God has not given us a spirit of fear (2 Tim. 1:7). Perfect love casts out fear (1 John 4:18). When we fear—and speak at the same time—what we say will come out wrong and may get us into serious trouble.

1. Abraham, telling people that his wife was his sister

Abraham journeyed to Egypt, and knowing how beautiful his wife, Sarah, was, he ordered her to say that she was his sister—so both of them would be spared. Abraham feared that someone would kill him in order to have her. So she did what he commanded. It worked for a while. She was taken into Pharaoh's palace, where she was safe, while Abraham prospered. But God stepped in. The Lord inflicted serious diseases on Pharaoh and his household because of Sarah. Pharaoh somehow knew that God had caused these diseases and knew that Sarah was Abraham's wife: "Why didn't you tell me she was your wife?" (Gen. 12:18). Abraham and Sarah mercifully were spared. They would never know what God Himself might have done had they trusted Him. Years later Isaac made the same mistake, repeating the error of his father (Gen. 26:7–22).

Speaking out of fear comes from assuming God is not going to look after us—so we speak in unbelief. It is the folly of self-protection. The truth is, God stepped in for both Abraham and Isaac. He will for us, too. But when we give in to unbelief and speak, thinking we are justifiably protecting ourselves, our sin has a way of backfiring on us.

2. Jacob, fearing his reunion with his brother, Esau

Jacob had not seen his brother in years. The last word Jacob heard about Esau was that Esau was hell-bent on getting vengeance upon him for stealing his birthright (Gen. 27:42–44). Jacob had lived in mortal fear all these years, knowing they would sooner or later meet up. The time had come. Jacob received the message: Esau "is coming to meet you, and four hundred men are with him" (Gen. 32:6). This news terrified Jacob. He cried to God, "Save me, I pray, from the hand of my brother Esau, for I am afraid he will come and attack me, and also the mothers [Rachel and Leah] with their children" (v. 11).

Jacob divided the people who were with him into two groups. He commanded his servant to speak to Esau and tell him that all the animals present were to be a gift to Esau. Fearing for his life, Jacob thought that bribing Esau with hundreds of goats, camels, donkeys, and cows would pacify him (vv. 14–18).

It was at that time Jacob experienced one of his greatest visitations from God—when he wrestled with the angel who changed his name to Israel (vv. 22–28). One would have thought this was all Jacob needed. Surely such an experience would increase his faith and take away all fear! But no. He was still filled with anxiety. He divided the children in such a manner that showed he was still scared nearly to death (Gen. 33:1–2).

But when they actually met each other it was a most happy moment. They hugged each other and wept. Esau was grateful for the offer of the gifts but said, "I already have plenty, my brother. Keep what you have for yourself" (Gen. 33:9). But he eventually accepted the gift.

But there is more. Whereas Esau wanted to have more fellowship with his brother, Jacob in panic made up a story that got him away from Esau as soon as possible, hoping never to see him again. All Jacob did with Esau was to feign words of praise, gratitude, and devotion, and promised to meet up shortly. The truth is, Jacob wanted out of there—and took off immediately (vv. 12–17).

Jacob, in fact, lost the victory that should have been his. Esau turned out to be the gracious man. Jacob, God's chosen vessel, disgraced himself before God and the angels by his fear over nothing. "Do not fret—it leads only to evil" (Ps. 37:8).

3. Moses, feeling inadequate for the task God called him to

It was such an honor to be called to deliver the people of God from Pharaoh's bondage. Moses may well have appreciated this, but all he did was to argue back: "O Lord, I have never been eloquent. . . . I am slow of speech and tongue. . . . Please send someone else to do it" (Exod. 4:10, 13). God did not like that. "The LORD's anger burned against Moses," but God offered to let Aaron assist him (v. 14).

The fact that God was displeased with Moses's response indicates that the role of Aaron was Plan B. We will never know what might have occurred in ancient Israel had Moses not given in to fear. What we do know is that Aaron turned out to be a real problem again and again, cooperating with the rebellion that surfaced with the Israelites.

Many people think that it is modest and noble to avoid Christian service due to a feeling of inadequacy. But when it is sheer unbelief, the Holy Spirit is quenched. What God calls us to do He enables us to do. St. Augustine prayed, "Command what Thou wilt, and give what Thou commandest." When we say no to the calling of God, whatever our reason, our tongue will witness against us.

We may think that our words do not matter if only God hears us. But He is the most important witness of all! We should care most of all what He thinks about our reaction to His Word.

Chapter Six

LOSING YOUR TEMPER

A fool gives full vent to his anger, but a wise man keeps himself under control.

—PROVERBS 29:11

SPEAKING PERSONALLY, I FEAR THIS IS WHERE I have sinned the most over the years. I have shouted at my wife and my children more often than I dare think about. I know that the deacons at Westminster Chapel feared my temper, certainly in my earlier days there. Some of them bravely told me so. I know what it is to speak sharply to a slow waitress in a restaurant, an incompetent clerk in a store, or to people moving too slowly in the line at a supermarket. I have been impatient with people in the vestry at Westminster Chapel—right after preaching a good sermon! Instead of demonstrating gentleness, I would look at my watch and wonder how long these people were going to keep asking inane questions. Undoubtedly one of my greatest weaknesses has been that I do not "suffer fools gladly" (2 Cor. 11:19, KJV).

The man who controls his temper is greater than a powerful warrior "who takes a city" (Prov. 16:32). "Wisdom makes one wise man more powerful than ten rulers in a city" (Eccles. 7:19). Remember that wisdom in controlling the tongue is knowing what to say next and what not to say.

Sometimes there is a thin line between righteous anger and losing your temper. The difference is that when it is righteous anger you do not lose control, as seen in the following biblical examples.

1. Moses, in the manner in which he addressed the people for their grumbling

The Israelites longed to be back in Egypt—and blamed Moses for everything they didn't like, including there being no water to drink. Moses was certainly put on the spot. He went into the Tent of Meeting and fell facedown, and the glory of the Lord appeared. Then the Lord explicitly told Moses, "*Speak to that rock* before their eyes and it will pour out its water" (Num. 20:8, emphasis added). But instead of speaking to the rock—which was Christ (1 Cor. 10:4)—he spoke to *them.* He scolded them, "Listen, you rebels, must *we* bring you water out of this rock?" (Num. 20:10, emphasis added). He had taken things personally despite God's gracious word and felt challenged to prove his leadership. Instead of speaking to the rock, he verbally attacked the people. He then struck the rock twice with his staff. Although water gushed out, Moses had a lot to answer for. God immediately said to him,

"Because you did not trust in me enough to honor me as holy in the sight of the Israelites, you will not bring this community into the land I give them" (v. 12).

Moses took their criticism personally and lost control by turning on them rather than simply speaking to the rock: "Because they provoked his spirit, so that he spake unadvisedly with his lips" (Ps. 106:33, KJV). The NIV says, "Rash words came from Moses' lips."

Moses was probably the greatest leader of people in world history. But he was not perfect. The people wore him down; he could take it no more. Instead of speaking to the rock—which would have defied natural explanation so that God would get all the glory for the water that gushed out—he struck it, making it something he did. I think that his rash words with the people may have caused the anointing on him to lift—which is why he did not carry through with the Lord's command.

2. Paul, before the Sanhedrin

As Paul began to testify, the high priest ordered those near Paul to strike him on the mouth. Paul retorted, "God will strike you, you whitewashed wall! You sit there to judge me according to the law, yet you yourself violate the law by commanding that I be struck!" (Acts 23:3). Those near Paul said, "You dare to insult God's high priest?" (v. 4). Then Paul mellowed, "I did not realize that he was the high priest; for it is written: 'Do not speak evil about the ruler of your people'" (v. 5).

I am aware that many interpreters of this account would find no fault in Paul's behavior. I disagree with them. To be sure,

Paul is my greatest hero. But he wasn't perfect. Luke shows that he was clearly seen by those around him as having insulted the high priest. What he said, even if the man had not been the high priest, is not a display of meekness. Paul implicitly admits this. It was not his finest hour. But from that point on he was brilliant; the anointing clearly did not lift from him. I am sure that he repented for calling the man in charge (even if he did not know it was the high priest) a "whitewashed wall." I know that I have done this sort of thing; then I lowered my voice—and quietly repented before the Lord in order to have clear thinking from then on.

Chapter Seven

LUST

Each one is tempted when, by his own evil desire, he is dragged away and enticed.

—JAMES 1:14

SEXUAL SIN, WHETHER IT BE ADULTERY OR premarital sex, usually begins with *words*. A person may be inwardly tempted. But once a word is uttered that registers what is going on inside, all hell can break loose. As long as one keeps quiet about it, the devil is kept at bay. But once either the man or the woman lets it be known that there is a sexual attraction going on, it is like a spark igniting a forest fire. The tongue is "a fire," and James was not merely referring to one's losing his or her temper (James 3:6).

1. David, sending for Bathsheba and getting her to sleep with him

At the very height of his kingship, when David was enjoying every success imaginable, with nothing going wrong and everything going right, he did something that was so very, very foolish. Some think he was bored with success. But it is apparent that he should have carried through with what kings did at a time like that—go to war (2 Sam. 11:1). But he didn't. He let others do it. He stayed behind. What we know is, David got up from an afternoon nap and noticed from his balcony a woman bathing. Some want to blame her for making herself available, but this is sheer speculation. The culprit was King David. If only he had been turned away the moment he saw her.

But no. He spoke. His tongue got him into more trouble than he would ever imagine. One could not blame him if he was attracted to a woman washing herself, as the King James Version of the Bible puts it. And the Bible even makes a point to say she was "very beautiful" (2 Sam. 11:2), as if to make one sympathize somewhat with David. Indeed, he would have been forgiven for thinking, *Wow, that is one beautiful woman.* After all, men are normally aroused by sight. But he gave in. He should have done the responsible and mature thing—immediately turn away from looking at her and get on with being the good king that he was. Until then.

But, sadly, he spoke, ordering someone on his staff to get him information that was none of his business. He said something like, "Find out who that beautiful woman is." It was a fatal attraction. What followed—moments later, days later, years and years later—could have been avoided but for the tongue. It is so often what gets us into trouble. Having ordered someone to find out who she was, he got back the reply: "She is a married woman, her name is Bathsheba, and her husband is Uriah the Hittite, one of your soldiers in the battle."

The king could not have had a greater warning than that. It left him utterly without excuse. But David was not content with the information that she was a married woman. He sent for her to come to his residence.

She came to him, he slept with her, and she returned home. What both of them may have thought would be merely a one-off afternoon affair ended in one of the greatest tragedies described in the Old Testament. She sent word back a few weeks later: "I'm pregnant." This was certainly not good news. But David had what seemed to be an easy solution. He sent for Uriah, pretended to want information about how the battle was going, and then told him to take a few days off and spend time with Bathsheba, his wife. This seemed to him a benign way to cover his sin. But Uriah was an honorable man, having what some might call an overly scrupulous conscience. He refused to sleep with his wife, knowing his fellow soldiers were risking their lives in the battle. David even ate and drank with him, trying to get him drunk. Uriah still would not see his wife.

The unthinkable followed. King David instructed his general Joab to place Uriah in the front of the battle so Uriah would be mortally wounded. It happened precisely that way. To cover his sin of adultery, David thus resorted to murder (2 Sam. 11:3–17).

It is often said that whereas men are sexually aroused by sight, women are aroused by tender *words*, and sometimes flattery (although it can happen the other way around, too). The point is, whatever nonverbal exchange might be taking place— by communication through the eyes, for example—it is when one *speaks*, and he or she reveals desire for the other person, that sexual excitement is often caught by that other person, and the passion cannot often be controlled.

But someone will say, "If one lusts—and Jesus calls this adultery in the heart—one might as well carry out the physical act." Wrong. That's the devil talking. Jesus was trying to teach the Pharisees a lesson in the nature of sin. (See Matthew 5:27–30.) The physical act of adultery is infinitely worse than the lust of the heart. In any case, a good number of competent evangelical scholars believe that the original Greek shows that what was adultery in the heart was *trying to create lust in the other*. The sin was causing the other to lust, whether by words from the man or provocative dress by the woman. But though this is adultery in the heart and needs to be repented of, it is the physical act of adultery that brings disaster, the heartache, the pain, the regret.

Billy Graham recently said that it seems the devil gets 75 percent of God's best servants through sexual temptation. It is inflamed with words—flattery, flirting, and seducing through conversation.

If there is anybody reading these lines, man or woman, and you are involved—even potentially—in an affair, I would come to you right now and say to you, STOP IT! Break it off. Now. The day will come, and it will surely come, that you would give a thousand worlds if you could turn the clock back to this very moment.

2. Samson, revealing his secret to Delilah

Samson was famous for his tremendous strength. I doubt any human being before or since had strength as he did. But it did not have a natural explanation; it was solely by the Holy Spirit. On one occasion, for example, "the Spirit of the LORD came upon him in power so that he tore the lion apart with his bare hands as he might have torn a young goat" (Judg. 14:6). On another occasion he caught three hundred foxes and tied them tail to tail in pairs, fastened a torch to each pair of tails, lit the torches, and let the foxes loose in certain fields of the Philistines—which destroyed their crop (Judg. 15:4–5). He once struck down one thousand men with a jawbone of a donkey (v. 15).

The Philistines were determined to find out the secret of Samson's strength. Their intelligence revealed that Samson's weakness was, simply, women. He even frequented prostitutes, and the word spread (Judg. 16:1–2).

By the way, what is your weakness? We all have them. It is sometimes referred to as one's "besetting sin," or "the sin that so easily entangles" (Heb. 12:1). You can be sure that Satan has a computer printout on your DNA, your lifestyle, your habits, and your weaknesses. He will work overtime through those who can get to you and tempt you in the area of your weakness. Be aware of this. "Clothe yourselves with the Lord Jesus Christ, and do not think about how to gratify the desires of the sinful nature"

(Rom. 13:14). The KJV puts it this way: "Make not provision for the flesh, to fulfil the lusts thereof."

In the meantime, Samson fell in love with a woman whose name was Delilah. The rulers of the Philistines asked her to see if she could lure him into revealing the secret of his great strength. They promised her money if she would comply. She did. She pressed him day after day to reveal the secret of his strength. He kept making up stories, refusing to tell her.

But finally, after she nagged him "day after day until he was tired to death," he gave in (Judg. 16:16). He told her everything. "No razor has ever been used on my head.... If my head were shaved, my strength would leave me, and I would become as weak as any other man" (v. 17). Shortly after that, while he was asleep on her lap, she arranged to have his hair cut. His strength left him. When the Philistines seized him, they gouged his eyes and took him down to Gaza. Binding him with bronze shackles, they put him in prison. It would not have happened had he been able to control his tongue.

What if you had an unusual anointing and there was a secret to it? It is only between you and God. Would you be able to keep quiet about it? Would you cave in to revealing the secret under pressure? It could be that your particular weakness is not sexual temptation, but, say, needing the admiration of certain people. Would you value the anointing more than having anybody know the secret to it? The psalmist said, "The LORD confides in those who fear him" (Ps. 25:14). The KJV reads, "The secret of the LORD is with them that fear him." Most people cannot keep secrets. I have long felt that God would do far more for us if we could keep quiet about it. God may be pleased to give you an unusual and extraordinary anointing—on the condition that you were to keep quiet about it.

God was merciful to Samson in the end. While he was in prison, his hair began to grow. When they brought him into a large place to make fun of him, he asked to be put where he could feel the pillars that supported the temple. Three thousand Philistines were present. Samson prayed, "O Sovereign LORD, remember me. O God, please strengthen me just once more, and let me with one blow get revenge on the Philistines for my two eyes" (Judg. 16:28). Bracing himself against the pillars that supported the temple, he cried out, "Let me die with the Philistines!" (v. 30), and the temple came down on all the rulers and all the people in it: "Thus he killed many more when he died than while he lived" (v. 31).

Samson had a brief but strategic restoration in the end—at the very last. "All's well that ends well," said Shakespeare. And Samson's example holds out hope for those who have fallen and who may feel there is no chance of being used again. One of the next books I write will deal with this and will show how God does take fallen heroes and bring them back to repentance. It could therefore be said of Samson, when the future seemed hopeless, that God wasn't finished with him yet.

PART TWO

SUCCESS IN CONTROLLING THE TONGUE

The law of truth was in his mouth, and iniquity was not found in his lips: he walked with me in peace and equity, and did turn many away from iniquity.

—MALACHI 2:6, KJV

THESE WORDS IN MALACHI 2:6 DESCRIBE THE kind of life God required for priests in the Old Testament. These words are found on the tombstone of Jonathan Edwards (1703–1758), the man God sovereignly used in the Great Awakening in New England and the greatest theologian in American history. I would wish more than anything I can dream of that God Himself might make this claim about me after I am gone. Every minister should want these words to describe him or her.

It will be recalled that James says, "If anyone is never at fault in what he says, he is a perfect man" (James 3:2). And yet enjoying a measure of success in controlling the tongue on occasion does not mean you are perfect! I can assure you that you have not "arrived"—even if you go three days without an unguarded comment or if the problem of controlling the tongue is now behind you. Tongue control is only a temporary grace—given one day at a time and hour by hour, even when you are having a good day.

I don't mean to be discouraging. But a New Testament doctrine of sanctification is needed here. We need both a scriptural and a realistic understanding of biblical holiness. Any teaching that purports that you, before you get to heaven, can be totally sanctified—soul, spirit, body, and tongue—is unbiblical and misleading. People who are taught such a notion often get frustrated, even demoralized, by their attempts to maintain perfection.

I should know. I was brought up in a denomination that emphasized "entire sanctification" (based upon 1 Thessalonians 5:23), stressing in particular what was known as "two works of grace"—being "saved" (the first work) and "sanctified" (the second work). The second work was said to have eradicated the sinful, carnal nature. Many theologians in that denomination, it is only fair to say, came to alter that understanding. But I know what I myself was taught. I would go to the altar again and again to get the "second blessing" so that I did not lose my temper ever again—and finally experience control of the tongue. I never got it. I never met anybody who did! This would include my godly parents. They were as "good as they come," but they did not have what their church leaders told them they had. They might make excuses for their "faults," "errors," "mistakes"—they would never ever call them sin. They were sincere but misguided.

This book is not a treatise on the New Testament doctrine of sanctification. I have dealt with this in other books (you might take a look at my *Understanding Theology*, published by Christian Focus). But let me summarize what the Bible teaches about sanctification. I would define it as the process by which we become more and more like Jesus. But we never become totally pure and sinless in this life. However, we can certainly make progress. It is a daily exercise to fight the flesh and resist temptation—whether that temptation refers to pride, sex, fear, or tongue control.

In a word, we never become sinlessly perfect in this life. God saves sinless perfection for glorification when we are in heaven. In the meantime, we must daily mortify the deeds of the body, fighting against the world, the flesh, and the devil (Rom. 6:11–14). This we can certainly do because we are under grace. We must not go on in willful sinning that grace may abound (v. 1), but we are still loaded with imperfections and the proneness to come short of God's glory (Rom. 3:23). This is why we need the daily cleansing of Christ's blood (1 John 1:7). We have the Holy Spirit, moreover, to resist temptation and to grow in grace, thus manifesting the fruit of the Spirit in ever-increasing measure (Gal. 5:22–23).

Never being at fault in what one says, then, means perfection. James is obviously not expecting that of any Christian, as the verses following James 3:2 show. (We will examine these verses later in this book.) So the tongue is something you must live with, work with, and get victory over—little by little—every day. But one day at a time! It is terrific when you have a good day. It is very encouraging. But if you had a good day, I lovingly caution you: wait until tomorrow!

I know what it is sometimes to preach well, to come down from the pulpit with an inner confidence, and to say to myself,

"Well, at last I have learned how to preach." But when I feel like that for very long, here is what happens—nearly every time: I do so poorly the next time I am in the pulpit that I leave saying, "If that is the best I can do, I should get out of the ministry." So if you have a good day with tongue control, thank God for it, but don't be deluded that you have mastered the art of tongue control; you just might be a miserable failure the next day.

The truth is, however, we can improve. We do get better at it. The reward is worth the effort, I promise you. That is why I wrote this book! There is hope for us all! Success in controlling the tongue is something that we must pray for all the time. This book is designed to help.

This is a word that can indeed also apply to a preacher or a writer. We must learn to waste no words—whether in the pulpit or with the pen. I don't mean that I have tips on how to preach or write, but tongue control in our personal lives should have the effect of helping us to know when to stop preaching or writing. Some preachers seem never to know when to stop—and drive their hearers mad. I would rather quit when the congregation is wanting me to keep on preaching than keep preaching and have them say to themselves at the end of the sermon, "I'm sure glad that's over." So in writing. I pray the Holy Spirit will enable me to say all I need to say in this very book—and stop at the right time.

But this book is about everyday conversation. It is about not only showing self-restraint with the amount of words when you are in conversation (learning not to tire people out), but also about making the right choice of words with friends, relatives, spouses, fellow Christians, and people we run into all the time. "A man of knowledge uses words with restraint, and a man of understanding is even-tempered" (Prov. 17:27). I want this book to be a contribution to your knowledge—that it will make a definite, life-changing impact on your personal life.

We will now look at examples of those who had success in controlling the tongue. These will often include those very people already seen in this book as having failed! Only Jesus—our ultimate example—was perfect. But God is gracious and gives us moments and occasions when we get it right.

Chapter Eight

CLIMBING DOWN

The first to present his case seems right, till another comes forward and questions him.

—PROVERBS 18:17

IT IS NOT EASY TO ADMIT THAT YOU HAVE BEEN wrong. Nothing challenges big egos like being faced with the evidence that says, plainly, you were wrong! And then you have to climb down.

I have had to face this many times. I die a thousand deaths before I give in, you can be sure. I will hold out until the end—hoping against hope that *I was not wrong!*

The problem is often this. We may have taken a stand on a situation. People disagreed with us. It could be a decision about a person and what they did; it could be a theological point of view; it could be about a job, choice of a church, the value of a particular minister, directions in traffic, or who should be elected to political office; it might be the choice of where to spend a vacation. The list is endless.

I know of well-known church leaders—not to mention political leaders—who would not change their position simply because they put their point of view in print—or stated something publicly. We back ourselves into a corner and become defensive. It hurts to admit you got it wrong when a lot of people know what you said or did.

I had to do this publicly with the "Toronto Blessing." When I first heard that strange things were happening at Holy Trinity Brompton, a prominent Anglican church in London, I had little difficulty dismissing it all as the latest fad in one stroke. People being prayed for, falling on the floor, and laughing their heads off—surely this could not be God, I said. For one thing, I did not *want* it to be of God (that would be threatening, indeed), as I find that sort of thing highly offensive. For another thing, if it really were of God, it would have come to Westminster Chapel first! After all, we (not them) had borne the heat of the day; we had our prayer meetings; we were witnessing faithfully on the streets of Westminster; I had put my reputation on the line again and again. God would bless *us* before He would bless the Church of England (which I regarded as largely apostate). It would be a betrayal should God bless an upper-middle-class Anglican church with their posh, Etonian accents!

Immediately after I heard about these bizarre things taking place at Holy Trinity, I made a public statement about it from the pulpit at Westminster Chapel. I cautioned my people against it, although I did admit that church history indicates that God can do some awfully strange things to confound the sophisticated. So I took my stand.

I have described the process elsewhere (in my books *In Pursuit of His Glory* and *The Anointing: Yesterday, Today, Tomorrow*[1]), so I will simply say here that some weeks later I stood in the same pulpit at Westminster Chapel and said, "I was wrong," and that what was going on at Holy Trinity was indeed of God. I also encouraged people to go there and get prayed for. By the way, I have never been sorry I climbed down; it turned out to be one of the most important decisions I made in my twenty-five years at Westminster Chapel.

It feels good to admit we were wrong! Yes, it hurts our pride. And there will certainly be those who question our judgment and will always be suspicious of us for the rest of our lives. But the inner peace that comes from the Holy Spirit compensates a thousand times over for the embarrassment our "climb down" brought on.

There were people in the Bible who had to climb down, too.

1. Samuel, who thought that Eliab would be God's choice to be the next king

Samuel had come to the house of Jesse to anoint the next king of Israel. He looked at Eliab, Jesse's firstborn. In ancient Israel, the firstborn son always received double the inheritance. It was natural for Samuel to think Eliab was the one—he even said so: "He looked on Eliab, and said, Surely the LORD's anointed is before him" (1 Sam. 16:6, KJV). When a prophet with the stature of Samuel makes an utterance like that, imagine how thrilled and humbled both Eliab and Jesse were. But Samuel had jumped the gun.

God stepped in and said to Samuel, "Do not consider his appearance or his height, for I have rejected him. The LORD does not look at the things man looks at. Man looks at the outward appearance, but the LORD looks at the heart" (v. 7). As I say in *The Anointing: Yesterday, Today, Tomorrow*, Samuel was a type of "today's man," and to be on the cutting edge of what God is going to do in our own generation, we must be in continual readiness to admit our mistakes when, after all, we got it wrong. A prophet has to do this; a theologian has to do this; a church leader has to do this. A husband has to do this with his wife and family. A boss has to do this in the office. A political leader has to do this before a nation—if he has the humility to do so.

Jonathan Edwards taught us that the task of every generation is to discover in which direction the Sovereign Redeemer is moving, and then move in that direction. I, for one, do not want to miss what God is in. This means I must continually swallow my pride and be willing to correct past mistakes and failures—however great the stigma. Otherwise, any anointing I have will lift from me. It is my greatest fear that the anointing would be taken from me and I become yesterday's man.

Samuel went through all the sons of Jesse, seven of them, and was about to give up! "Are these all the sons you have?" he asked. Jesse admitted there was one more son—young David, tending the sheep—but Jesse for some reason did not seem very keen to waste time with him. But Samuel said, "Send for him; we will not sit down until he arrives" (1 Sam. 16:11). When David came in, the Lord instructed, "Rise and anoint him; he is the one" (v. 12). God frequently chooses sovereign vessels that you and I would overlook—all because of our prejudices. God loves to surprise us and especially select someone that we who are so traditional, erudite, and cultured will want to reject.

If you and I are going to be God's instruments in our time, we must be willing to climb down, admit our errors, throw our reputations to the wind, and worship God. The anointing we get in return is worth it all.

2. The prophet Nathan, having encouraged David to get on with his dream to build a temple

We saw earlier that the prophet Samuel had to climb down from a word he gave to Jesse. Another prophet, Nathan, had the trust of King David. David had conquered Jerusalem, brought the ark there, won every war he fought, and now was looking for more to do. He wanted to build a temple for the Lord.

> After the king was settled in his palace and the LORD had given him rest from all his enemies around him, he said to Nathan the prophet, "Here I am, living in a palace of cedar, while the ark of God remains in a tent."
>
> Nathan replied to the king, "Whatever you have in mind, go ahead and do it, for the LORD is with you."
>
> —2 SAMUEL 7:1–3

When a man with enormous prophetic stature talks like that, you take it seriously! God was certainly with David, there was no doubt about that; Nathan therefore apparently felt safe to tell him to get on with whatever was on his heart.

But before Nathan was permitted to go to sleep that night, the Lord came to him and told him, in so many words, to climb down from what he said to King David. (See 2 Samuel 7:4–16.) Then Nathan had the task of reporting the revelation that God said, "No, David, you can't build the temple after all," but David still accepted Nathan's latest word.

It smacks of transparent integrity when a person known to have a prophetic gift has the honesty and courage to say, "Sorry, I got it wrong." Few do this, I fear. They are afraid they will lose their authority if they take back what they said. So people like this make a choice: take back what they said, or lose their anointing. That should be an easy decision, but apparently it is not for some. The truth is, prophets are people. Not every word that comes from their lips is inspired by the Holy Spirit. But sometimes their followers think otherwise, and sometimes a prophetic person seems to want people to hang on to his or her every word.

Nathan must have been one of the greatest prophets of all time. He was a man of unusual prophetic gifting and also of tremendous courage. What follows is an example of how this same Nathan had to confront David with some of the most fearful words ever given from a prophet to a man in authority.

3. David, having been so self-righteous about the person described in Nathan's parable

We have already seen David's sin and attempted cover-up by having Uriah killed. Some time later God sent the prophet Nathan to David with a parable:

> There were two men in a certain town, one rich and the other poor. The rich man had a very large number of sheep and cattle, but the poor man had nothing except one little ewe lamb he had bought. He raised it, and it grew up with him and his children. It shared his food, drank from his cup and even slept in his arms. It was like a daughter to him.
>
> Now a traveler came to the rich man, but the rich man refrained from taking one of his own sheep or cattle to prepare a meal for the traveler who had come to him. Instead, he took the ewe lamb that belonged to the poor man and prepared it for the one who had come to him.
>
> —2 SAMUEL 12:1–4

After hearing this, David went ballistic. He "burned with anger" and declared, "As surely as the LORD lives, the man who did this deserves to die! He must pay for that lamb four times over, because he did such a thing and had no pity" (vv. 5–6).

Nathan replied, "You are the man!" and commenced to describe to David what David had done (and thought he got away with) in sleeping with Bathsheba and striking down Uriah. Then he prophesied to David, "The sword will never depart from your house, because you despised me and took the wife of Uriah the Hittite to be your own" (v. 10).

Self-righteousness is an exceedingly difficult sin to see in ourselves. Part of our inherited depravity from Adam is self-love and pride. We are quick to judge others but slow to see the equivalent sin in ourselves. Who would have thought that sins like adultery and murder would need a parable to make a person see his wrong! But sometimes the most heinous sins have a way of camouflaging our perception and causing us to miss seeing the most obvious maladies we have. That was David.

The only man in the Bible called a man "after God's own heart" (1 Sam. 13:14; Acts 13:22) was guilty of one of the most shameful sins and crimes in ancient Israelite history. But one of the proofs that he was indeed a man after God's own heart was his reaction to Nathan.

David climbed down. No defensiveness. No justification for what he did. He owned up to everything on the spot: "I have sinned against the LORD" (2 Sam. 12:13). He meant it and took to heart every word Nathan continued to say. It makes one think of a well-known TV evangelist who, when found out, said before the world, "I have sinned." But he immediately dug in his heels, and when his denominational authorities gave him instructions as to the way forward, he refused counsel. This is the way one becomes yesterday's man or woman.

God wasn't finished with David yet. True, there was a blight on his life and he was under a cloud that lasted a long time. But he continued to write psalms, and he was still used of the Lord. Let no one think that sin, however great, necessarily finishes you off. Enter into Psalm 51 and pray with David, admitting your guilt and asking for mercy, and know too the hope he had: "Then I will teach transgressors your ways, and sinners will turn back to you" (v. 13). Or as it is put in Psalm 130:4: "But with you there is forgiveness; therefore you are feared."

We have a big God—one who has provided a sacrifice for our sins in His Son Jesus Christ: "If we confess our sins, he is faithful and just and will forgive us our sins and purify us from all unrighteousness" (1 John 1:9). God has been appeased by the blood of His Son, and all we need do is to confess our sins to God, turn from them, and move on:

> Who is a God like you,
>> who pardons sin and forgives the transgression
>> of the remnant of his inheritance?
> You do not stay angry forever
>> but delight to show mercy.
>
> —MICAH 7:18

4. Naaman, having been offended by Elisha's instructions on how to be healed

Naaman, an army general under the king of Aram, was a leper. He was told that if he could get to the prophet Elisha, he would be healed. It took a lot of faith and humility for a man like this to come over into Israel—having also to clear this with the king of Israel—and ask to be healed by someone he did not know. The link was a young girl from Israel who was a servant to the general's wife. She kept saying to her mistress, "If only my master would see the prophet who is in Samaria! He would cure him of his leprosy" (2 Kings 5:3).

Naaman eventually found his way to Elisha's house. But Elisha did not even come out to greet Naaman. A general is not used to being treated like that. This was almost certainly a blow to his pride. Not only did the prophet Elisha not come out to meet Naaman, but he also merely sent a messenger to say to the general, "Go, wash yourself seven times in the Jordan, and your flesh will be restored and you will be cleansed" (v. 10).

Naaman was indignant. How dare Elisha treat him like that! As for the word the messenger actually sent, it was adding insult to injury. Wash seven times in the river Jordan! This must be some sort of a joke. So he refused to comply. He left in a rage. But he did explain how nothing went according to his expectation: "I thought that he would surely come out to me and stand and call on the name of the LORD his God, wave his hand over the spot and cure me of my leprosy" (v. 11). Even though Naaman was a Syrian, knowing virtually nothing of the ways of the God of Israel, he still thought he knew how the famous prophet would perform. He was not prepared to be treated in this manner. Nothing made sense. Not only that, but if he was to wash in a river, "Are not Abana and Pharpar, the rivers of Damascus, better than any of the waters of Israel? Couldn't I wash in them and be cleansed?" (v. 12).

God seems to delight not only in offending the sophisticated by the vessel He chooses but also in the *manner of ministry* as well. It certainly made perfect sense for Naaman to be cleansed by the rivers at home. Why ever not?

This is the kind of question people ask: "Why do I have to go to Toronto to be blessed?" "Why do I have to be prayed for by this or that person? Won't my own minister do as well?" "Why do I have to go to this particular church when there is one around the corner from where I live?" And if it should be a wealthy or famous person, they might say, "I want a personal audience with this person. I don't want to have to sit out in the audience like everybody else. Why should I take a chance risking my reputation?"

All these may seem reasonable questions. But it just happens that the God of the Bible has chosen the foolish things of the world to confound the wise, the weak things of the world to shame the strong. (See 1 Corinthians 1:17–28.) Like it or not, God said, "For my thoughts are not your thoughts, neither are your ways my ways.... [As a matter of fact,] as the heavens are higher than the earth, so are my ways higher than your ways and my thoughts than your thoughts" (Isa. 55:8–9). I know people who say, "If I become a Christian, it won't be in *that* church or through *that* minister," or, "If I let anybody pray for me it will have to be so-and-so—nobody else." I think God looks down and quietly passes over people who put those kind of demands on God.

I shudder to think where I would be today had I let my biases govern all my decisions over the years. I would have missed the most strategic moments of my life. Nearly fifty years ago I began to experience how God chooses servants that are utterly outside my "camp" to reach me. (See Hebrews 13:13.) He has been doing it ever since. Nothing can be more deadly than provincialism—when we live in our own narrow community and fancy that "if God is going to work, it will happen with us."

To their everlasting credit, Naaman's own servants went to him, probably with fear and trembling, and said, "If the prophet had told you to do some great thing, would you not have done it? How much more, then, when he tells you, 'Wash and be cleansed'!" (2 Kings 5:13). In other words, they were gently showing Naaman that he had nothing to lose.

He climbed down. He went down to the river and "dipped himself in the Jordan seven times, *as the man of God had told him*, and his flesh was restored and became clean like that of a young boy" (v. 14, emphasis added). Then Naaman and all his attendants went back to the man of God—this time they got to meet Elisha personally—and he said, "Now I know that there is no God in all the world except in Israel" (v. 15).

Naaman's tongue almost robbed him of one of the most extraordinary miracles in history.

5. Nathanael, after being biased about the city where Jesus lived

Philip, having just been converted, went to Nathanael and said, "We have found the one Moses wrote about in the Law, and about whom the prophets also wrote—Jesus of Nazareth, the son of Joseph." Nathanael wasted no time retorting to this news, "Nazareth! Can anything good come from there?" Philip replied, "Come and see" (John 1:45–46).

Some people are prejudiced over a particular person; others object to a particular place. In England the typical southern Englishman seems to feel a cut above the northerner—from York or Manchester. But in America the northerner often looks down on people (like me) from Kentucky or Tennessee! We get used to an accent or style and become set in our ways. A person from New York or New England cannot imagine that a person with a "hick" accent can have anything of substance to say!

But Philip insisted that Nathanael "come and see" for himself. It was good advice. Once Nathanael became willing to meet Jesus, something unexpected occurred: Jesus saw him coming and said of him, "Here is a true Israelite, in whom there is nothing false." Astounded, Nathanael replied, "How do you know me?" Jesus answered, "I saw you while you were still under the fig tree before Philip called you" (vv. 47–48).

Nothing is more calming to us than when we discover that God knows all about us. It gives a good feeling of trust, a feeling that we are cared for. God knew exactly how to cut across Nathanael's prejudice.

In the early days when I was at Westminster Chapel, a person came to hear me, dragging his feet, because his friends insisted on it. "I will never be blessed by an American," he said to them. It turned out that he had worked for some American bankers who had treated him unfairly. But he came. My sermon that day was on Jonah, when he was at sea in a storm and the sailors asked him, "Who are you?" and Jonah replied, "I am a Hebrew" (Jon. 1:8–9). Somehow my message tapped into that hostile man. He thought his friends told me all about him. He sat on the pew afterwards crying. God broke down the barriers.

He has to do that with all of us. None of us would climb down from our fixed position were it not for the sheer grace of God.

So Nathanael climbed down: "Rabbi, you are the Son of God; you are the King of Israel" (John 1:49). Had not friends said, "Come and see," and had Nathanael stuck to his guns, his life would never have been changed. His tongue almost kept him outside the kingdom.

6. Thomas, who vowed not to believe Jesus was raised from the dead unless he saw the nail prints in His hands

Thomas, one of the twelve disciples, was not present when Jesus showed Himself alive to the disciples. I personally think he believed their report, "We have seen the Lord!" (John 20:25). He knew they would not make up a story like that; they had been as discouraged over Jesus' crucifixion as he was.

I think he was just hurt. He felt cheated that he was not present when Jesus showed up. He was feeling sorry for himself and sulking, refusing to believe their account: "Unless I see the nail marks in his hands and put my finger where the nails were, and put my hand into his side, I will not believe it" (v. 25). Strong words. I would not encourage anybody to talk like that! God owes us nothing, and the person who demands empirical proof of the Bible before he becomes a Christian will almost certainly never believe. You cannot bluff God.

But Jesus knew Thomas. He remembered he was but dust (Ps. 103:14). A week later Jesus did turn up, and this time Thomas was present. Jesus singled out Thomas and graciously said to him, "Put your finger here; see my hands. Reach out your hand and put it into my side. Stop doubting and believe" (John 20:27).

Thomas climbed down. He said to Jesus, "My Lord and my God" (v. 28). Thomas got it right with his tongue that time! But Jesus was the gracious one. Jesus, by doing this, let Thomas save face. God is like that. He could, if He chose, hold our words against us—and pass us by completely. But He is gracious and gives all of us a second chance.

7. Ananias, as well as a number of Christians, not believing Saul of Tarsus was converted

Saul's conversion took place with no Christians witnessing it. The last thing that Christians knew about Saul of Tarsus was that he was dedicated to exterminating every Christian alive! The first to receive the news of Saul's conversion did not hear it from a Christian but from the Lord Himself.

Acts 9:11–14 tells the story. In a vision Ananias was simply told, "Go to the house of Judas on Straight Street and ask for a man from Tarsus named Saul, for he is praying" (v. 11). Ananias wanted to argue—or, at least, he doubted whether he was having an authentic vision from the Holy Spirit: "Lord...I have heard many reports about this man and all the harm he has done to your saints in Jerusalem. And he has come here with authority from the chief priests to arrest all who call on your name" (vv. 13–14). One sympathizes with Ananias. It is consoling to me that you can question the Lord as Ananias did when it seemed so extraordinary.

But the Lord replied, "Go! This man is my chosen instrument to carry my name before the Gentiles and their kings and before the people of Israel. I will show him how much he must suffer for my name" (vv. 15–16).

Ananias believed these words, climbed down, and went to Saul and prayed for him.

Christians everywhere were having the same problem. Rumors spread of Saul's conversion, but they thought it could be a setup. When Saul came to Jerusalem, "he tried to join the disciples, but they were all afraid of him, not believing that he really was a disciple" (v. 26). This time it was Barnabas who made the apostles see that Saul was truly converted.

All eventually believed and climbed down, and the church everywhere "enjoyed a time of peace" (v. 31). The church was never the same again.

Chapter Nine

IN THE PRESENCE OF AN ENEMY

You prepare a table before me in the presence of my enemies.

—PSALM 23:5

W HEN JESUS SAID, "LOVE YOUR ENEMIES" (Matt. 5:44), there was an underlying assumption that we would have them! There are, of course, degrees to which this is true. It could be a long-standing enemy that wants to destroy you, a neighbor who is always annoying, a rival who is jealous of you, or someone who is a temporary nuisance. But we all have them, sooner or later. Tongue control with a person like this is an extremely delicate test—and yet good practice for other areas of our lives. Jesus said that the one who is faithful in what is least will also be faithful in much (Luke 16:10).

I was preaching on total forgiveness in Northern Ireland, and a minister came up to me afterwards and said, "Can your wife be your enemy?" I was slightly taken aback, having never been faced with that question before! But I answered: yes. When there are difficulties in marriage, the spouse often appears as an enemy. How one copes with words with one's husband or wife is crucial, but there is equally an opportunity for practicing tongue control in all relationships.

1. David, running from King Saul

The Bible says that David behaved himself wisely in all his ways (1 Sam. 18:14, KJV). This is stated right after his victory over Goliath, which gave him a new relationship with King Saul. Killing Goliath was both the best thing and the worst thing to happen to David at the time. It was good—it gave him favor with the king and the people. But his anointing was a severe threat to the king. The refrain, "Saul has slain his thousands, and David his tens of thousands" (v. 7), made Saul go ballistic. He used up more energy in trying to hunt down and destroy David than he did fighting Israel's enemy—the Philistines. This is how perverse jealousy can cause one to be.

Behaving oneself wisely means making the right decisions, but mainly it refers to self-restraint with words. For the next twenty years David would learn self-control regarding the tongue. It was part of his preparation for the kingship. The great English preacher Charles Spurgeon once said, "If I knew I had twenty-five years left to live, I would spend twenty of it in preparation." Dr. Martyn Lloyd-Jones once said to me, "The worst thing that can happen to a man is to succeed before he is ready." King Saul succeeded before he was ready, and he ended in utter failure. God was determined that David, a man after His own heart, would not succeed until he was ready.

You may be wondering, "Why do I have to wait so long before God will use me?" Or perhaps you ask, "Why is God taking so long to do what He promised?" The answer probably has to do with God overruling in your life in a manner that keeps you from being successful before you are ready. He is looking out for you; He knows your frame and remembers that you are "dust" (Ps. 103:14). So be encouraged. God is dealing with you in the same exact manner He handled David. It is because He loves you too much to let you succeed before you are ready.

David began at once to practice restraint with the tongue. King Saul offered his daughter in marriage to David. David shrewdly responded as if he did not see through the king's motive: "Who am I, and what is my family or my father's clan in Israel, that I should become the king's son-in-law?" (1 Sam. 18:18). That was the first hint that David was learning to survive away from home. It was the first proof that God's hand was on him. David knew that Saul hated him. From that moment on, it was part of David's preparation for the kingship to develop skills he never knew he had: the skills to survive when someone is out to get you.

Having an enemy is good for us. It keeps us on our toes. I can honestly say that my own anointing has been increased and refined by the presence of an enemy. I learned to see the enemy as God's way of preparing me. My first reaction was, "Why, Lord?" But I came to see why: it was for my good—to develop character, strength, perseverance, and total forgiveness. I could never have written *Total Forgiveness* were it not for the fact I had to forgive utterly and totally those who wanted to hurt me.[1]

On two occasions David had opportunity to get personal vengeance on the king—and he turned down the chance both times. "I will not lift my hand against my master, because he is the LORD's anointed," he said to King Saul (1 Sam. 24:10). David was steadfast in not giving the slightest occasion for the king to fault him. On the second occasion David refused to let his men destroy Saul because David knew that Saul's future and his own future was in God's hands: "The LORD himself will strike him; either his time will come and he will die, or he will go into battle and perish. But the LORD forbid that I should lay a hand on the LORD's anointed. Now get the spear and water and jug that are near his head, and let's go" (1 Sam. 26:10–11).

Turning down the second opportunity to destroy Saul was also a testimony to his loyal followers. These men could never forget this. It showed David's true character. When we have enemies, we also usually have some followers. How we behave toward our enemies in the presence of our followers is important. It is a testimony to what we are really like. David would pen those words from what is perhaps his most beloved psalm: "You prepare a table before me in the presence of my enemies" (Ps. 23:5). How we behave toward our enemy will be noted by all who look on. It is a part of God refining us because He isn't finished with us yet.

2. The Israelites, refusing to speak under the evil threat of Sennacherib

The king of Assyria sent his forces into Jerusalem to address Hezekiah the king and the common people who sat on the wall. These soldiers shouted insults to Israel's God and to the king. They hoped to cause a revolt among the ordinary people: "Now do not let Hezekiah deceive you and mislead you like this. Do not believe him, for no god of any nation or kingdom has been able to deliver his people from my hand or the hand of my fathers. How much less will your god deliver you from my hand!" (2 Chron. 32:15).

Hezekiah sent word to Sennacherib's men to please not speak in Hebrew to the people. Hezekiah was fearful that the people would weaken and give in. It was the greatest national crisis during the reign of King Hezekiah.

But King Hezekiah need not have worried. It was a grand and historic moment: "But the people remained silent and *said nothing* in reply, because the king had commanded, 'Do not answer him'" (Isa. 36:21, emphasis added). It was a wonderful moment. It was a beautiful sign of unity in Israel that not one person succumbed to Sennacherib's men. Shortly afterwards God supernaturally defeated Israel's enemies, and Sennacherib's own people cut him down (Isa. 37:36–37).

Satan will always try to persuade the people of God to interact with him and negotiate with him. The Bible says, "Resist the devil, and he will flee from you" (James 4:7). When you feel pressured to speak, remember this account in Scripture. In such cases, when the exact word is not given to you, the best thing to do is to *say nothing.*

3. Moses, having to face double opposition—from his own people and from Pharaoh

There is a sense in which every church leader is in continual threat of twofold opposition—from within and without. The greater enemy, of course, is the world out there that needs to be confronted and converted. We must never forget the greater enemy and never fall into the trap King Saul fell into—to become more concerned about his personal enemy David than he was the Philistines. The devil would prefer that we are more concerned about opposition to our personal leadership than we are about marching into Satan's territory to bear witness to our Lord Jesus Christ.

But every Christian leader knows what it is to have opposition from within the circle of those you are leading. There will be those, almost always, who question your leadership—your wisdom, your decisions—and sometimes it is a bit of jealousy behind the whole thing you have to contend with.

We saw earlier that Moses lost control of his temper on an important occasion toward the sunset years of his life and ended up having to forgo entering the Promised Land. But he still had some forty years of impeccable leadership, showing all of us who are leaders the best way to handle those you lead. He was a pioneer leader, but he eventually became almost too exalted among the Israelites. I sometimes wonder if God permitted Moses to make a big mistake at last to keep everybody from idolizing him.

Sometimes I think God even lets a leader fail lest people admire him or her too much!

Moses experienced every conceivable kind of opposition. He knew what it was for his following to turn from hot to cold in their attitude and loyalty to him. When he first appeared to the children of Israel as their appointed and anointed leader, he announced what God revealed to him and performed signs before them. The people believed. And when they heard that the Lord was concerned about them and had seen their misery, they bowed down and worshiped. It was a good beginning.

But after Moses's first confrontation with Pharaoh to immediately emancipate all the people and allow them to leave Egypt, Pharaoh, instead of giving in to Moses's command, put out a decree for the people to find their own straw for making bricks— and keep up the same quota. As a result of the added hardship, the people of Israel turned not against Pharaoh but Moses: "May the LORD look upon you and judge you! You have made us a stench to Pharaoh and his officials and have put a sword in their hand to kill us" (Exod. 5:21).

Moses's reaction: he said nothing back to them but turned to the Lord. God has big shoulders. I have often marveled at David's words: "I pour out my complaint" to the Lord (Ps. 142:2). This is what leaders must do. Instead of snapping back or complaining to their people, they must pour out their complaints to God. God can cope with the pressure.

One of the greatest tests for Moses was having both his own people and the armies of Pharaoh coming against him simultaneously. How many of us who are leaders could cope well with that?

Following the Passover, the children of Israel had been given permission to leave Egypt. As they came to the edge of the Red Sea, they assumed that they were finally rid of the bondage of Pharaoh, but here came his armies marching toward them as the children of Israel were trapped with nowhere to go. If that wasn't enough, Moses's own people turned against him and said, "Was it because there were no graves in Egypt that you brought us to the desert to die? . . . It would have been better for us to serve the Egyptians than to die in the desert!" (Exod. 14:11–12).

Moses might have retorted, giving these ungrateful and unworthy people a piece of his mind, but he controlled his tongue. He had presence of mind and answered the people, "Do not be afraid. Stand firm and you will see the deliverance the LORD will bring you today. The Egyptians you see today you will never see again. The LORD will fight for you; you need only to be still" (vv. 13–14).

The truth is, despite this brave face, Moses was scared. I say this because in the very next verse, the Lord said to Moses, "Why are you crying out to me?" (v. 15). This can only mean that Moses had just cried to the Lord, even if it was only in his heart. It is as though there might have been a verse that said, "Moses cried to the Lord," right after he said those gracious words to the children of Israel.

God stepped in and told Moses, "Raise your staff and stretch out your hand over the sea to divide the water so that the Israelites can go through the sea on dry ground" (v. 16). Moses did, and they did. And the rest, as they say, is history.

4. The counsel of Jesus, when called to testify before governors and kings

Jesus said:

> Be on your guard against men; they will hand you over to
> the local councils and flog you in their synagogues. On my
> account you will be brought before governors and kings as wit-
> nesses to them and to the Gentiles. But when they arrest you,
> do not worry about what to say or how to say it. At that time
> you will be given what to say, for it will not be you speaking,
> but the Spirit of your Father speaking through you.
>
> —MATTHEW 10:17–20

I will never forget the first time I took serious notice of this passage. I was pastor of a small church in Ohio where my teaching was brought under question. They claimed not to have a creed or statement of faith—"only the Bible," they said to me. But when I preached from the Bible, they rejected me—at least a large number of them did. I was called on the carpet by the ministers in the area.

On the day I was to face their charges, I opened my Bible, and unexpectedly these words from Matthew 10:17–20 leaped out at me. I knew then that God would be with me and that what I was having to do was similar to what Jesus said would happen. I was amazed at myself that night; I hardly spoke! But what I said nobody refuted. The ministers urged the people to try being nice and to get along with one another. I left a few months after that, but I can never forget how God saw me through that evening.

I quoted these words to Yasser Arafat when I saw him just a month or so before he died. I told him that I claimed those words every time I visited him (five times) and that what I said to him was not me but Jesus! He smiled and seemed to accept what I said. He knew too that I never entered the political arena; I stayed entirely with the gospel of Jesus and His death on the cross for our sins.

The point is this: when we need words in an emergency or on special occasion, God is capable of giving us the exact words we need. If one does not carry an agenda on such an occasion, not thinking in advance what to say but letting the Spirit take control, it is amazing what comes out of our mouths!

In other words, Matthew 10:20—"it will not be you speaking"—is the only time I know of where we are *guaranteed* grace to control the tongue to that degree. I wish I could claim that verse twenty-four hours a day, seven days a week, but, alas, Matthew 10:20 is only promised for "emergency grace." In any case, Matthew 10:20 shows that God certainly knows the right word! Indeed, "from the LORD comes the reply of the tongue" (Prov. 16:1).

5. Stephen, speaking before the Sanhedrin

The Holy Spirit speaking through His servant (Matt. 10:20) is exactly what was in full operation on the occasion when Stephen, having been maligned and falsely accused, was brought before the Sanhedrin. (See Acts 6:11–14.) Most of Acts 7 is Luke's report of Stephen's defense. It is a brilliant survey of Old

Testament history with particular reference to a long tradition of opposition to the latest move of God.

Stephen could not have spoken like that had he not also known his Old Testament. What was happening was the Holy Spirit bringing to his remembrance what he had learned (John 14:26). Let no one think that he or she can stand up and speak like this if the knowledge is not first imbedded in the heart and mind! We may think that if we are Spirit-filled, God will pour knowledge into our heads. If only! I would have to say kindly that if we are empty-headed before we are Spirit-filled, we will be empty-headed afterwards. There *is* place for Scripture memorization, reading good books, and sitting under sound teaching. When the Holy Spirit comes down on a people in power, it will be on those who took the trouble to *learn* when it may not seem inspirational or easy.

6. Jesus, when forced to testify before the chief priest, Herod, and Pilate

I have long been fascinated by Paul's words that our Lord Jesus, testifying before Pontius Pilate, "made the good confession" (1 Tim. 6:13).

Jesus never said anything wrong the whole of His life. He was sinless in thought, word, and deed. So it is in a sense redundant to say that He spoke the words from the Father when standing before Herod and Pilate. All He ever did was this: "The Son can do nothing by himself; he can do only what he sees his Father doing, because whatever the Father does the Son also does" (John

5:19). Therefore the Spirit of the Father was always the explanation for His perfect words.

And yet Jesus gives us the perfect example of tongue control in the presence of the enemy before Herod, the high priest, and Pilate. There are two things that contributed to this "good confession":

1. The timing of His silence
2. The choice of His words

As a sheep before her shearers is silent, so he did not open his mouth.

—ISAIAH 53:7

When Jesus was brought before Herod, the latter "plied him with many questions, but Jesus gave him no answer" (Luke 23:9). It demonstrates that He had no fear whatsoever.

It takes a lot of confidence and courage to say *absolutely nothing*. That utter silence was what partly made Jesus' testimony before the authorities so stunning. It demonstrated His total peace, confidence, and self-control.

But Jesus ended up answering the high priest because He faced a different situation with him:

The high priest stood up and said to Jesus, "Are you not going to answer? What is this testimony that these men are bringing against you?" But Jesus remained silent. The high priest said to him, "I charge you under oath by the living God: Tell us

if you are the Christ, the Son of God." "Yes, it is as you say,"
Jesus replied.

—MATTHEW 26:62–64

Why did Jesus speak to the high priest? He had to. He had
put Himself under the Law (Matt. 5:17; Gal. 4:4) and therefore
had no choice. The Law said, "If a person sins because he does
not speak up when he hears a public charge to testify regarding
something he has seen or learned about, he will be held responsible" (Lev. 5:1). This is why He spoke to the high priest. I had
not made the connection between Matthew 26:64 and Leviticus
5:1 until Richard Roe, a deacon at Westminster Chapel, shared
this with me.

Regarding Pilate, Jesus maintained silence with him for a
while. When asked, "Where do you come from?" Jesus gave no
answer. But when Pilate said, "Don't you realize I have power
either to free you or to crucify you?" Jesus chose to answer: "You
would have no power over me if it were not given to you from
above. Therefore the one who handed me over to you is guilty of
a greater sin" (John 19:9–11).

In answering these words to Pilate, Jesus affirmed the state.
It is the New Testament position that the authorities that exist
are ordained of God (Rom. 13:1). Jesus was an example of how
we are to respect law and government, even if we do not always
agree with who is in power. Paul called His witness a good
confession.

Chapter Ten

DIGNIFYING THE TRIAL

Consider it pure joy, my brothers, whenever you face trials of many kinds.

—JAMES 1:2

IN THE FALL OF 1979, LESS THAN THREE YEARS after starting my ministry at Westminster Chapel, I began a series of sermons on the Book of James. I planned this series for several weeks. We had a six-week vacation, part of which was at Disney World. We had been the year before, as it happens, and I wasn't particularly looking forward to going back. But our children were eager to do so, so of course we went. Being there had one minor consolation. I recalled the best pizza I ever ate when we were there the previous year, at a pizza parlor in Kissimmee, Florida. I promised everybody that I would get pizza from there again.

After we checked into our motel, we journeyed to the pizza place, about six blocks away. Louise, TR, Melissa, and I put in our orders. I ordered the "deluxe" with everything imaginable on it, including anchovies. After a good while the pizza was still not ready. I went to the counter and asked about it. They did not have my order. A new man came on a shift, "So what do you want?" he said—not bothering to apologize. I did not exactly radiate the love of Jesus, but I grudgingly called the family up, and we ordered again. It finally came, and when I paid, I did not smile; neither was tongue control in operation. We had been there about forty-five minutes.

When we came outside it was pouring rain—a real tropical downpour. We dashed to the car, getting wet, but we all thought it was worth it—those pizzas were going to be so good! When we got back to the motel, Louise, TR, and Melissa took their pizzas and ran to the room (we were parked in front of it). When I got out, I stepped into a foot of water. I opened the back door and water poured on my pizza—and the sack that was carrying it was drenched. The whole pizza fell out into the water—the whole thing: sausage, pepperoni, peppers, cheese, mushrooms, onions, and anchovies!

My verbal response to this was not my finest hour.

If I was to eat anything, I had no choice but to go back—and reorder. I immediately thought of having to face the man to whom I was not the epitome of Christlikeness.

But an amazing thing happened during the six-block drive to the pizza restaurant. My mind immediately went to James 1:2: "Count it all joy when ye fall into divers temptations" (KJV).

I said to myself, "Either what I preach is true or it isn't," and I wanted my earliest sermons on James to launch the series in good fashion. The phrase *dignify the trial* came into my head. I immediately determined to dignify that trial (it seems so silly now), but it was literally a life-changing moment for me and the beginning of an era that lasts to the present day in which I have sought as faithfully as possible to dignify every trial God allowed me to have.

I apologized to the man at the pizza place. I was so ashamed. He made another, and he didn't even charge me!

I began to think how many years had gone by (I was forty-four then) when I did nothing but murmur, complain, and grumble through every trial that ever came my way—however great or small. I felt so ashamed. But I vowed that day—and I have sought hard every day since, not always succeeding, to keep that vow. As I write these lines I am seventy. I still make every effort to focus on dignifying any trial God allows to come my way. Laugh if you will, but it all began with the pizza incident!

People hear our words. My family hears my words. The angels hear our words. God hears our words.

Dignifying the trial means to accept any trial graciously as being a gift of God, to go through it all without complaining, and letting it last as long as necessary to accomplish God's purpose in it. All trials do end! When the trial is over, we either pass or fail in the sight of God. When God says, "Well done," at the end of the trial, it means not only that sweet affirmation but also an increased anointing! What determines our grade? Our words.

1. Abraham, when told to sacrifice his son Isaac to the Lord

Abraham is called the father of the faithful (Rom. 4:11). He was Paul's chief example for justification by faith but also for receiving an inheritance. Both teachings are in Romans 4. I happen to believe that the key to the next great move of God on the earth is the Book of Romans, especially chapter 4. Abraham was justified by his faith in the promise (Gen. 15:6), but he received an inheritance by accepting that his true heir would come from Sarah's womb (Rom. 4:18–21).

But there was more testing for Abraham. Few people have suffered like Abraham. But suffering is not for nothing. The greater the suffering, the greater the anointing. One day God told Abraham to sacrifice his son Isaac (Gen. 22:2). I cannot imagine a trial greater than that. Abraham not only obeyed, but he also dignified this unthinkable trial by his words. Sometimes God asks us to do things that make no sense at all at the time. Abraham had witnesses—two of his servants—before whom he would also bear witness. But he did not say to anybody what all was happening where they were going—or why; he was quietly obeying the Lord.

Knowing there would be a sacrifice of some sort by their taking wood for the burnt offering, Isaac asked, "Where is the lamb for the burnt offering?" This must have been the hardest moment of all for Abraham. He could have lost control of his emotions and words here. But he didn't. Abraham answered, "God himself will provide the lamb for the burnt offering, my son" (v. 8). There was no talk like, "How could God do this to me?" "This is not fair." "This doesn't make sense." There was no sulking. He simply obeyed. That is dignifying the trial.

Abraham fully intended to carry through with God's order. But he was stopped by the Lord Himself at the last moment: "Do not lay a hand on the boy.... Now I know that you fear God, because you have not withheld from me your son, your only son" (v. 12).

The consequence of this was one of the greatest spiritual experiences that ever can be given to a human being on this planet—namely, to have God swear an oath to you: "I swear by myself... I will surely bless you and make your descendants as numerous as the stars in the sky and as the sand on the seashore" (vv. 16–17).

When we bless the Lord by tongue control, He blesses us by telling us what we want to know—and a thousand times more than we could dream of. Dignifying the trial is a promised route to those who desire a greater walk with God and a greater anointing of the Holy Spirit on their lives.

2. Leah, who learned to dignify her trial with words

Leah was Jacob's unwanted wife. He was tricked into taking her as his wife by his uncle Laban. (See Genesis 29:16–30.) As such, Leah was the woman he never loved or appreciated. She was a rival to her beautiful sister, Rachel, who was very much loved by Jacob. Leah had one compensation: she could bear children when Rachel could not.

But one of the strong motives she had for wanting children was the hope that, at long last, Jacob would love and appreciate her. When she gave birth to Reuben, she said, "It is because the

LORD has seen my misery. Surely my husband will love me now" (v. 32). But he apparently didn't.

She gave birth to another son, Simeon, and said, "Because the LORD heard that I am not loved, he gave me this one too" (v. 33).

Her fourth child was Levi. When he was born she said, "Now at last my husband will become attached to me, because I have borne him three sons" (v. 34). But there is no indication that having these three sons made any difference with Jacob. He loved Rachel.

God was wanting to teach Leah that He loved her, even if Jacob did not. The entire ordeal was part of God's preparation for Leah—and also the church—that He is behind all that happens to us.

She had one more son—Judah. I find her words so moving, I can hardly read them without coming to tears: "This time I will praise the LORD" (v. 35). Those words went up to heaven like sweet incense. She dignified her trial with words that reveal she had come to terms with what was not going to happen—winning her husband's love—and what had already happened—having the Lord love her so much.

Which of the sons do you suppose became the greatest blessing to Israel down the road? Rachel eventually gave birth to Joseph and Benjamin, but Leah's two sons that gave the church the ultimate gift were Levi, from which sprang the Levitical priesthood, and Judah, the tribe that produced Israel's Messiah and our Lord and Savior, Jesus Christ.

Leah's blessing, although it was not what she wanted, turned out to be the greater blessing to the church. When she said, "This time I will praise the LORD," she could not have known that God had strategically placed her in a position to bless His people through her more than ever. And she remains an example to all of us, especially unloved women, who can learn to dignify the trial through words.

3. Eli, upon hearing most disquieting words about his legacy

Eli was the high priest at the time Samuel was born. When Samuel was a little boy, he heard from God one night but did not know what to make of it at first. When God called Samuel, he answered, "Here I am," but ran to Eli, not thinking God would speak to him directly. But Eli replied that he had not spoken and told the young Samuel to go back to bed.

But it happened again; the Lord called, "Samuel!" and Samuel got up and went to Eli and said, "Here I am; you called me." But Eli said again, "I did not call; go back and lie down."

But when it happened a third time, Eli—to his everlasting credit—recognized the movement of the Holy Spirit and ordered Samuel, "Go and lie down, and if he calls you, say 'Speak, LORD, for your servant is listening'" (1 Sam. 3:9). And Samuel went back to bed.

Eli is one of the unsung heroes in the Old Testament. I used to talk about him with Dr. Martyn Lloyd-Jones, one of my predecessors at Westminster Chapel. "I always liked him and felt for him," Dr. Lloyd-Jones used to say to me. Eli had brought up two sons, destined from birth to be priests, but both of them went badly wrong. They were a grief to the aging Eli. (See 1 Samuel 2:22–25.)

When Samuel returned to bed that night:

The LORD came and stood there, calling as at the other times, "Samuel! Samuel!" Then Samuel said, "Speak, for your servant is listening."

And the LORD said to Samuel: "See, I am about to do something in Israel that will make the ears of everyone who hears of it tingle....I will carry out against Eli everything I spoke against his family—from beginning to end. For I told him that I would judge his family forever because of the sin he knew about; his sons made themselves contemptible, and he failed to restrain them. Therefore, I swore to the house of Eli, 'The guilt of Eli's house will never be atoned for by sacrifice or offering.'"

—1 SAMUEL 3:10–14

Those were awful words to have to hear. But Eli heard them because he demanded that little Samuel tell him every word, which Samuel did, hiding nothing from him. And yet it became a brilliant moment for Eli. It showed there was something good left in the dear old man after all, for he dignified this enormous trial with these words: "He is the LORD; let him do what is good in his eyes" (v. 18). His sons died a short time later in battle. The Philistines captured the ark of God, and when Eli heard that the ark was taken, he fell and died at the age of ninety-eight (1 Sam. 4:17–18).

The best way we can dignify a trial—however heavy it may be—is by words that affirm the wisdom and judgment of God. God likes it when we bless Him in this manner. First, that we recognize God at work—"It is the Lord." And secondly, that we bend the knee: "Let him do what is good in his eyes." If all else that has proceeded is bad, and very bad, speaking like that is not a bad way to end.

4. King David, during his exile

One of the most sublime examples of dignifying a trial with words was when King David, leaving Jerusalem in humiliation, was cursed by a man called Shimei. Shimei pelted David with stones, despite David being guarded. As he cursed, Shimei shouted, "Get out, get out, you man of blood, you scoundrel! The LORD has repaid you for all the blood you shed in the household of Saul, in whose place you have reigned. The LORD has handed the kingdom over to your son Absalom. You have come to ruin because you are a man of blood!" (2 Sam. 16:7–8).

This would be pretty tough to have to listen to. It was probably the worst thing David would want to hear at a time like this, if only because he would be the first to admit there was a bit of truth in these words.

How did David dignify this trial with words? He said to his officials (who could have gotten immediate vengeance), "My son, who is of my own flesh, is trying to take my life. How much more, then, this Benjamite! Leave him alone; let him curse, for the LORD has told him to. It may be that the LORD will see my distress and repay me with good for the cursing I am receiving today" (vv. 11–12). Shimei continued on and on with his cursing, but David controlled his tongue.

5. Jehoshaphat, praising God in the midst of the battle

This king of Judah was given some disquieting news: "A vast army is coming against you from Edom" (2 Chron. 20:2). Alarmed, Jehoshaphat resolved to seek the Lord, and he proclaimed a fast for all Judah. The people all responded. Jehoshaphat was given a prophetic word: "You will not have to fight this battle.... Do not be afraid; do not be discouraged. Go out to face them tomorrow, and the LORD will be with you" (v. 17).

What was Jehoshaphat's response? He took the prophetic word seriously and went to his people: "Listen to me, Judah and people of Jerusalem! Have faith in the LORD your God and you will be upheld; have faith in his prophets and you will be success-ful" (v. 20). At that point the king did something most extraor-dinary; he appointed men to *sing* to the Lord and to praise Him "for the splendor of his holiness as they went out at the head of the army, saying, 'Give thanks to the LORD, for his love endures forever'" (v. 21).

This is one of those video replays I look forward to seeing when I get to heaven. *As they began to sing and praise,* the Lord stepped in with a particular strategy by which Judah defeated the enemy. The lesson for us: God loves praise. Thank Him in the darkest hour. Trust the word He has given. This way He does the fighting for us.

6. The apostles, after they left the Sanhedrin

Peter and the apostles had been put in jail for preaching the gospel, but they were miraculously set free and commenced preaching again in the temple courts (Acts 5:17–20). They were arrested again and warned about teaching in the name of Jesus. Peter and the apostles replied, "We must obey God rather than men!" (v. 29).

A Pharisee named Gamaliel stood up in the Sanhedrin and cautioned the Jews not to be too hard on them—lest they be fighting against God. His speech persuaded them, but they still had the apostles flogged, commanded them not to speak in the name of Jesus, and then let them go (vv. 33–40).

Here are some of the most moving words in the Book of Acts: "The apostles left the Sanhedrin, rejoicing because they had been counted worthy of suffering disgrace for the Name" (Acts 5:41). I love the way the King James Version put it: they rejoiced "that they were counted worthy to suffer shame for his name."

The Jews probably thought they had taught Peter and his friends a lesson, that the strong words and flogging would succeed in keeping them quiet—and make them feel ashamed.

They could not have known that the opposite was true. The apostles couldn't believe their luck, if I may put it that way. They regarded suffering for the shame of the name of Jesus as a very high honor—they did not feel worthy of this! But they were getting it!

You might question, therefore, if this is dignifying the trial. It was something they welcomed. That makes it no trial. But of course it was a trial. It hurt. But the privilege of rejoicing in this transcended the pain and disgrace so that they were honored to have this.

A ninety-year-old lady once said to a friend of mine years ago, "I have been serving the Lord so long that I can hardly tell the difference between a blessing and a trial."

When you dignify a trial with rejoicing, not only is it a blessing, but it also leads to greater honor and blessing. The early church was just beginning at that time. Far, far more was to come. So too with us. Welcoming a trial, rather than rejecting it, augurs well for our future. We prove that we accept it graciously by what we say.

7. Jesus, accepting God's will in Gethsemane

The writer of Hebrews was partly referring to Jesus in Gethsemane when he said, "He offered up prayers and petitions with loud cries and tears.... He learned obedience from what he suffered" (Heb. 5:7–8). The latter phrase is something I do not profess to understand; I just believe it.

At any rate, Jesus was the supreme example of dignifying a trial. While in Gethsemane, anticipating the cross, His agony was so great that "his sweat was like drops of blood falling to the ground" (Luke 22:44). But it was in Gethsemane that He settled it finally that there was no other way to proceed but by the cross. He prayed, "My Father, if it is possible, may this cup be taken from me. Yet not as I will, but as you will" (Matt. 26:39).

Dignifying the trial is accepting the wisdom, verdict, and will of God without complaining. The prayer of Jesus in Gethsemane lets us know that we don't wish for a trial. In the Lord's Prayer we are told to pray, "Lead us not into temptation" (Matt. 6:13). The Greek word *peirasmos* is translated either temptation or trial. We don't pray to enter into temptation or trial, but we dignify such if it must come.

However, Jesus apparently hoped to have a little company with

Him during this ordeal. He took Peter, James, and John with Him. I take the view that He was lonely, feeling the anguish, and somehow hoped that the pain might be slightly lessened by having these three men with Him as on previous occasions.

But they slept through it all. He gently rebuked them, "Could you men not keep watch with me for one hour?" (Matt. 26:40). But they went back to sleep. When He went through this the third time, He came to terms that both Gethsemane and the crucifixion would be experienced by Him utterly alone. I am touched by the way the King James Version puts it in Matthew 26:45: "Sleep on now, and take your rest." However much He wanted to have them alongside, He knew He had to give this wish up.

He did not let them lose face. He simply said, "The Son of Man is betrayed into the hands of sinners. Rise, let us go!" (vv. 45–46). There was no self-pity, no grumbling, only dignity. Not only was He our sinless substitute in His death, but He was also our perfect example on how we are to live our lives and control the tongue.

We have seen seven examples of how to dignify our trials by controlling our tongues. Many of these men faced not only the trials of everyday life but also trials where their lives or the lives of their loved ones were hanging in the balance. They are examples of how we can rely on God to give us what to say at times when we are at our weakest. Now we will see what it is to forgive totally with our choice of words.

Chapter Eleven

TOTAL FORGIVENESS

A further reason for forgiveness is to keep from being out-smarted by Satan; for we know what he is trying to do.

—2 CORINTHIANS 2:11, TLB

THE BEST PREPARATION AND TRAINING FOR tongue control is practicing total forgiveness. Total forgiveness is the quickest way to ensure that the Holy Spirit is not grieved (Eph. 4:30–32), and when the *ungrieved* Spirit of God indwells us in greater and greater measure, the art of tongue control is more likely to be developed in us.

1. Joseph, when he revealed his identity to his brothers who had betrayed him

Because of dreams the Lord gave him (Gen. 37:5–11), Joseph always knew that one day his brothers would bow down to him. Because of their jealousy and hatred toward him, they sold him to the Ishmaelites, never expecting to see him again. But twenty-two years later Joseph's dreams were perfectly fulfilled. He had even become prime minister of Egypt, and these brothers had to come to Egypt to buy food. Joseph immediately recognized them, but they did not recognize him. He spoke through an interpreter. But the moment came when he could bear it no longer and decided to reveal his identity to them.

He always assumed he could look at those brothers and say "Gotcha!" Then he could throw the book at them and see them punished. But a new Joseph had emerged. He had totally forgiven them. How do we know?

First, he ensured that nobody would ever know what they did to him. He made everybody but the eleven brothers leave the room (Gen. 45:1). Behind closed doors he revealed who he was. He made sure nobody—ever—would find out what his brothers had done. Total forgiveness is *not telling anybody* what people have done to you. The way we normally "punish" those who hurt us is to make sure people know what "they" did to us. We try to get even by destroying their credibility—telling as many as we can what they did. We cannot bear that people would admire those who have hurt us.

Joseph would not let them be afraid of him. "Come close to me," he urged them, knowing they were terrified of him (vv. 3–4). He would not even let them feel guilty: "Do not be distressed and do not be angry with yourselves for selling me here" (v. 5). Most of us want to make sure the people feel guilty—and feel very sorry—before we forgive them.

He let them save face: "It was not you who sent me here, but God" (v. 8). He protected their egos, their self-esteem—even covering up for them to make them feel better. Joseph even protected them from their dark secret, namely, their letting their father, Jacob, think a wild animal had killed Joseph. He would not let them tell their father what really happened (vv. 9–11).

Finally, Joseph's forgiveness was something that lasted. Seventeen years later Jacob died. The brothers panicked and feared that Joseph would at last get vengeance on them. Never! He demonstrated that he still forgave them (Gen. 50:15–21). Total forgiveness is a "life sentence"; we do it as long as we live.

How did the brothers know Joseph forgave them? *He said things* that indicated there was no grudge, no bitterness. His *words* made *them* feel forgiven. They were thrilled. You only verbalize forgiveness, however, when the people need and want it. If they don't want it, you still must forgive them. But don't tell them in this case. Never say, "I forgive you," unless you know for sure it is what they yearn to hear from you. Otherwise they will resent it and accuse you of pointing the finger. Total forgiveness is articulated in such a manner that shows there is no bitterness in you whatsoever. For more details, see my book *Total Forgiveness.*

2. Moses, interceding before God on behalf of a people who rejected his leadership

I have said that Moses was the greatest leader of people in human history. And here is partly why. It was not merely his ability. He was a man who practiced total forgiveness. The Spirit of

God was in him *ungrieved*. This is why he had constant two-way communication with God.

An opportunity was handed to Moses by God on a silver platter that most leaders I know would have taken with both hands. God said to Moses, in so many words, "Moses, this is a sorry lot you have for a following. They are not accepting your leadership or Mine. I have decided to wipe them all out entirely and start all over again with you, and together we will build a new nation." (See Numbers 14:11–12.)

I would hate to think what I might have done had God said that to me in any of the churches of which I have been the minister. This includes all six churches I have led: (1) Church of the Nazarene in Palmer, Tennessee; (2) Fairview Church of God, Carlisle, Ohio; (3) Lauderdale Manors Baptist Church in Fort Lauderdale, Florida; (4) Blue River Baptist Church in Salem, Indiana; (5) Calvary Baptist Church in Lower Heyford, Oxfordshire, England; and (6) Westminster Chapel in London, England. I have had opposition to some degree in every single one of these churches. When it became very difficult, had God said to me what he said to Moses, I would not want you to know what would have come to my mind! I may well have taken God up on His offer.

But not Moses. No! He thundered back:

Then the Egyptians will hear about it! By your power you brought these people up from among them. And they will tell the inhabitants of this land about it. They have already heard that you, O Lord, are with these people.... If you put these people to death all at one time, the nations who have heard this report about you will say, 'The LORD was not able to bring these people into the land he promised them on oath; so he slaughtered them in the desert.' …In accordance with your great love, forgive the sin of these people.

—NUMBERS 14:13–19

I call that greatness. I would have to say that this moment was probably the greatest example of true greatness recorded by God or man in all human history. Greatness is not success or fame. Greatness is accepting the worst possible conditions and dignifying God through it all. I think of the words of Psalm 106:23: "So he said he would destroy them—had not Moses, his chosen one, *stood in the breach* before him to keep his wrath from destroying them" (emphasis added).

This is why God trusted Moses with so much authority, power, favor, and fame. To the degree we forgive totally will be the degree to which God entrusts us with a greater anointing. By the way, what do you suppose happened then? God forgave them!

Moses was not concerned about his personal ego or how *he* would look. He was concerned about the honor of God's name— and how the peoples of the earth would look at God.

3. Stephen, interceding for his killers just before he died

We had a brief look in chapter 9 at Stephen's anointing of speech before the Sanhedrin. I did not mention how Stephen's face was aglow "like the face of an angel" (Acts 6:15). We pointed out Stephen's grasp of Israelite history and how he used the moment to warn us that there is not only continuity with the blessing of God in history, but, sadly, there is also continuity with opposition to what God is in. There are two kinds of heritages, you might say.

When I had opposed the "Toronto Blessing" and listened to Ken Costa, churchwarden of Holy Trinity Brompton, tell me what was happening in his church, I suddenly had a strange feeling that I myself was about to fill out one more chapter in opposing the latest movement of the Spirit. *O Lord*, I thought, *please don't let me do this*. As soon as I saw that, I climbed down. The thesis of Stephen's reply to the Sanhedrin was precisely this.

I have marveled at Stephen's anointing, one of the original seven deacons—an example for every layman and every church leader in Scripture. What was the explanation for such ostensible radiance, power, and wisdom? I think I know. It is seen in Stephen's final seconds. As he was being stoned—a horrible way to die—Stephen's very last words were these: "Lord, do not hold this sin against them" (Acts 7:60).

Many of us, knowing that we are to pray for our enemies, will pray something like, "Lord, I commit them to You." I think God must be annoyed at such a prayer. The way He wants us to pray for those who have hurt us, however unjust they were, is that they would be let *off the hook*, that they will be blessed rather than cursed. That is what God asks us to do. When we do that, we demonstrate total forgiveness.

Stephen was also emulating our Lord Jesus Christ in His final moments. We therefore look at one more example of this kind of graciousness.

4. Jesus, praying for those who crucified Him

The most frequent criticism I receive from my book *Total Forgiveness* is my point that you must not wait until those who have hurt you repent or are sorry before you forgive them. These people want to say that we surely are not required to forgive people who have not repented first! I reply: nine out of ten people you ever have to forgive don't even think they have done anything wrong! So what are you to do? Go to them and point out how wrong they are? Hardly.

All four of these examples show, one at a time, that we are not allowed the luxury of waiting until they repent first. First, Joseph told the brothers "do not be angry with yourselves." Second, the children of Israel were not the slightest bothered over their rebellion when Moses prayed for them. Third, how sorry do you suppose these Jews were who were stoning Stephen?

So when Jesus prayed for those who crucified Him, how much repentance do you find at His cross? They laughed, and they scoffed: "Come down now from the cross, that we may see and believe" (Mark 15:32). "He saved others...but he can't save himself!" (Matt. 27:42). In fact, not only did they not repent, but also they were so sure they were right in doing this that they said, "Let his blood be on us and on our children!" (v. 25).

Jesus's response to all of this: "Father, forgive them, for they do not know what they are doing" (Luke 23:34). I agree with Dr. G. Campbell Morgan, one of my predecessors at Westminster Chapel, who said he expects to see in heaven the very people who drove in the nails. I would go further. I think when we get to heaven we will find that those who were converted at

Pentecost included many of these people who were active in Jesus's demise.

It takes minimal grace to forgive when people are sorry: "A gentle answer [soft answer—KJV] turns away wrath" (Prov. 15:1). Even coldhearted and wicked people can find it easy to forgive when the person is truly sorry. So forgiving people when they are sorry is no evidence whatsoever of the Spirit of God in you. But when you forgive them when they are *not* sorry—or when they don't even think they have done anything wrong, that shows grace indeed. That is what Moses, Stephen, and Jesus did. It is what we are required to do. And don't be surprised that God answers our prayer and forgives them—and lets them off the hook! "Oh, no," you may say. Oh, yes! That is the point!

We have a gracious God: "Be merciful, just as your Father is merciful" (Luke 6:36). This is true godliness. Not how plainly you dress, what movie theaters you don't attend, what things you give up, or how often you go to church; it is total forgiveness and being merciful just as God is.

It is our *words* that indicate whether we are bitter or loving. This is why Jesus said, "For by your words you will be acquitted, and by your words you will be condemned" (Matt. 12:37). You may have evil thoughts. Yes, we all have them. But we don't have to *say* them. "You might as well say what you think," some keep saying. Wrong. It is our tongues that get us into trouble. Controlling the tongue is the goal.

And likewise it is the *tongue* by which we bless people and honor the Lord.

PART THREE

THE TROUBLE WITH THE TONGUE

*We all stumble in many ways. If anyone is never at fault in
what he says, he is a perfect man, able to keep his whole body
in check.*

—JAMES 3:2

EVERY MISTAKE I HAVE EVER MADE, EVERY SIN I
have ever committed, and every sense of guilt that continues to
give me grief and pain can be traced to my own tongue.

But I am encouraged by James's word, "We *all* stumble in
many ways." James was the brother of our Lord (Gal. 1:19), or, to
be technical, half-brother. He was without question the "big gun"
in the early church. His word was law, no doubt because he was
seen by all as Jesus's brother. In any case, it is encouraging to me
that he said what he did about not being perfect—that all of us,
himself included, stumble in many ways.

James's opening statement in his discourse on the tongue,
therefore, immediately disarms all of us, setting us free from
unnecessary guilt, and thus lets us know that perfection, though
we should regard it as a valiant goal, is not realistically expected
by our gracious heavenly Father: "He remembers that we are
dust" (Ps. 103:14). God does not want us to beat ourselves black

and blue because we are not perfect. The best of God's servants in Scripture have had both successes and failures when it comes to tongue control. Only Jesus was perfect.

The word translated "stumble" in the New International Version is from the Greek *patio*, which means, "to slip," "to sin," "to fall," or "to offend." James's point that "whoever keeps the whole law and yet *stumbles* at just one point is guilty of breaking all of it" shows that he is talking about sin (James 2:10, emphasis added). Sinning with the tongue, however minute it may seem at first, has the potential to grieve the Holy Spirit seriously and cause unthinkable damage both to others and to ourselves.

We therefore have a mandate to deal with our tongues. The fact that we are not perfect and are not expected to be perfect is no warrant from God to settle for imperfection so as to neglect this matter. As a matter of fact, we are warned in no uncertain terms of the grave consequences of not making every effort to control our tongues. We are fools if we do not take the Word of God seriously and apply James's teaching to our lives.

As 1 Corinthians 13 is known as the "love" chapter of the Bible, and Hebrews 11 being the "faith" chapter of the Bible, so is James 3 the "tongue" chapter of the Bible. We need to look carefully at what the Holy Spirit has to say throughout the Bible generally and especially through James.

However, I want us also to look at other scriptures that deal with this subject as firmly as James did. What follows is so important that, just maybe, it could save lives, marriages, jobs, ministries, relationships, and careers. It would not surprise me to learn that this came to you in the nick of time.

Chapter Twelve

THE TONGUE ON THE WAY TO CHURCH

Save me, O LORD, from lying lips
  and from deceitful tongues.
What will he do to you,
  and what more besides, O deceitful tongue?

—PSALM 120:2–3

THESE WORDS ARE FROM THE FIRST PSALM OF Ascent. I have often wondered why, right at the beginning of this section (Psalms 120–134), we are given this word about the *tongue*. In a sense it is rather strange. Why would the psalmist plunge into this kind of subject when the ancient people of God were on their way to worship God in Jerusalem?

The Psalms of Ascent were sung by ancient Israelite pilgrims three times a year. They were sung on their way *up* to the three feasts of Jerusalem, which they were required to attend. The word *ascent* comes from the Hebrew word that means "going up." I have written a book called *Higher Ground* that deals with the fifteen Psalms of Ascent.[1] No matter where the ancient Israelites journeyed from, they had to go *up to Jerusalem* because this amazing city is 2,500 feet above sea level.

This psalm has to do with God getting our attention. What does God have to do to get our attention—even your attention? The funny thing is, the very thing that tends to put us off God is the very thing He uses to bring us back to Him!

The psalm may be seen as one that the pilgrims sang when they realized what needed to happen to them before they worshiped God properly. God had to bring distress to get their attention. "I call on the LORD in my distress, and he answers me" (Ps. 120:1). God uses adversity—or whatever causes distress—to get our attention. It drives us to our knees. God does what He has to do to get us to call on Him as we should.

I love the way Jonah 2:1 reads in the King James Version: "Then Jonah prayed." The previous verse says that the Lord provided a great fish to swallow Jonah, that he was inside the fish three days and three nights: "*Then* Jonah prayed." And, oh, how he prayed!

What does it take to get you to pray? By the way, how much do you pray? How much time do you spend in prayer? Children spell "love" T-I-M-E. What if God measures our love for Him by how much time we have for Him?

The first line in the first of the Psalms of Ascent therefore refers to calling on the Lord in distress. Perhaps it was distress that catapulted the pilgrims into making the journey up to Jerusalem. Maybe they did not want to go. They called on the

Lord in distress, and He answered! And so now they are on their way up to Jerusalem in obedience to God's word.

I like to think of it as being comparable to going to church. God wants His people never to forsake the assembling of themselves together (Heb. 10:25). The Hebrew Christians in the first century were discouraged and were getting out of the habit of meeting together. So likewise do we sometimes rebel at going to church. We think of various reasons not to go—and we feel quite right about it. But God has a way of getting our attention and showing us we need to meet with His people.

DIVERTED FROM WORSHIPING GOD

Louise and I attend a little church in Key Largo, Florida. In their weekly bulletin are these words: "Our church family is a group of imperfect people who have been brought together by the grace of God to worship Him, to be reminded of His forgiveness, and to find out what He wants us to do in this world."

The Christian isn't perfect; no church is perfect. But we need to be there.

But have you noticed how—on the way to church—*the tongue* makes an attempt to spoil the whole thing? There is shouting, arguing, bickering, murmuring, defensiveness, and the pointing of the finger—have you noticed it? Well, you are not alone. It is so typical and so frequent. *Satan does not want you to go to church.* He knows how to attack and to get us frustrated and angry at the very time we ought to be worshipful and full of anticipation.

Could this be why the psalmist mentions the tongue right at the beginning of the Psalms of Ascent? Take, for example, people coming from Galilee. It was a three-day journey. Today, I drive it in three hours. But not then. And when a group of people are going to be living close together for three days, all kinds of tensions can set in. They begin annoying each other. Perhaps this is why the tongue is put right at the beginning of these psalms.

One form of distress God uses to get our attention is caused by the deceit of others. The origin of the psalmist's distress appears to be that he was criticized unfairly. That is enough to divert you from worshiping God. Criticism is painful, even if it is true. If a person begins a sentence, "I say this in love"—watch out! But the psalmist was the victim of a deceitful tongue.

The psalmist had either been lied *to* or lied *about*. What is a lie? It is the postponement of the truth that will eventually come out. It is only a matter of time before the truth will come out. I guarantee it.

So relax. Lower your voice. Leave the lies to God. "'It is mine to avenge; I will repay,' says the Lord" (Rom. 12:19). But it is still disconcerting when a lie is used by the devil to direct your attention away from God. It is equally true that God uses all this to get our attention so we will turn to Him as we should.

In any case, on our way to worship, the devil loves to use lies and deceit.

Bad things often happen when something good is supposed to happen—or is about to happen. Worshiping God is always good and right. We therefore should not be surprised when the devil enters the picture. And what is his instrument? Surprise, surprise.

It is the tongue. The devil can do nothing without God's permission. God allows the devil to go so far but no further.

When you are lied about, it is a great opportunity for strength of character. You tell what you are when you are under fire. And there is nothing so intense as the heat of a deceitful or lying tongue. My advice (if you can take it): do not respond; focus on worshiping God. Keep going up to Jerusalem; go on to church. Get there, and worship there.

ALWAYS THINK "GARLIC"

In another psalm, David, when worshiping God and praying that his prayer be set before the Lord like incense, said, "Set a guard over my mouth, O LORD; keep watch over the door of my lips" (Ps. 141:3).

One of my favorite places to eat in London was a Middle Eastern restaurant. I went there so often that the chef once offered to prepare a special dish, noting that I love garlic. He took a large tomato, cut it several ways, then put a truckload of garlic and onions in the tomato, soaking it in oil and vinegar, and let it set for fifteen minutes. It was indescribably delicious. When I arrived home, Louise said, "What on earth have you eaten?" I explained. But all night long she kept asking me to roll over and face the other direction. The next morning I brushed my teeth, gargled, and did everything I could to get the odor off my breath. Nothing worked. Wherever I went, I did my best to keep my lips sealed rather than knock people over from my bad breath.

It taught me a lesson. When tempted to speak, always *think garlic*. It helps me keep my mouth shut. I am reminded of those haunting words: "When words are many, sin is not absent, but he who holds his tongue is wise" (Prov. 10:19).

It's a good thing to remember on the way to church. Or anywhere else.

Chapter Thirteen

ASKING FOR TROUBLE

Not many of you should presume to be teachers, my brothers, because you know that we who teach will be judged more strictly.

—JAMES 3:1

LONG BEFORE I FELT THE DEFINITE CALL OF GOD on my life to be a preacher, it was drummed into me, "Don't do it unless you are called by God." I don't know whether my old pastor knew about Spurgeon's warning—"If you can do anything else, do it"—but I do know I was told that the ministry is not for everybody, only those truly called of God.

Whereas Paul said that if anyone aspires to be a bishop, or overseer, he desires a "noble task" (1 Tim. 3:1, "good work," KJV), James clearly puts obstacles in the way of one who is thinking along the lines of going into the ministry.

If you wonder why James refers to being a "teacher" rather than "preacher," it is because every preacher was supposed to be a teacher. You might make a distinction between the two, which I could do, but the main thing to remember is that we who have the responsibility of dealing with God's Word—whether we be evangelists, pastors, prophets, or preachers—are expected to know what we believe and how to make it clear to those who are under our leadership. Any high profile among the people of God means that you are going to be judged by a different standard than others. Unfair? That is the way it is.

STRICTLY JUDGED—MORE REQUIRED

Some people aspire to the ministry because they see it as glamorous. Some think it is prestigious. Others go into it because they can't find a good job doing anything else. I think of George Bernard Shaw's famous words: "He who can, does. He who cannot, teaches."[1]

In seventeenth-century England, the best minds chose the ministry. This is not only because Oxford and Cambridge were originally set up when *theology reigned*, but also because the minister was to be very highly educated—the people expected it. When you examine the ministers, vicars, and priests who became clergy in the Church of England, you find they were the "top of the line." Today the best minds seem to go into areas of study like physics, medicine, or science. One should pray that this would change, that the most able people would want to go into the preaching or teaching ministry—that the church would be led by the most brilliant people.

But on one inflexible condition: that they are called by the Holy Spirit. One of the worst things that can happen to a person is to enter into the preaching or teaching ministry and not be called of God. It is a sure recipe for burnout and an eventual change of career. Most people who sit in the pews have no idea what it is like to be in full-time ministry. It ain't all fun, I can tell you, and the only thing that keeps a person sane who is in this kind of calling is knowing that God put him or her there.

Perhaps you know about *The Peter Principle* by Laurence J. Peter, the thesis being that every person is promoted to the level of his or her incompetence.[2] That may be true, but it is assuring to know that the Holy Spirit never promotes us to the level of our incompetence. "As thy days, so shall thy strength be" (Deut. 33:25, KJV). God will not lead you to do what you can't do. Just be sure you are being led by God Himself!

James gives a sobering but sensible reason for avoiding the ministry, if you can: those who are in the ministry will be *judged more strictly*. What does this mean? It basically means that those who are in the teaching or preaching ministry—whatever gives one a higher profile with the people of God—will not get away with lack of tongue control to the degree others might do. As Dr. O. S. Hawkins says, "Teachers will be judged more strictly if their works do not match their words."[3] This is for two reasons:

1. The people will judge you more harshly.

Regarding the first, once you are called into Christian ministry, like it or not, you are put on a pedestal in the eyes of the people. People will perceive you differently and consequently expect better behavior—with particular reference to the tongue. You may say, "I am no different than others." True. But you are *expected* to be different. "That's not fair," you may say.

James's reply to you would be this: don't even *think* about the teaching or preaching ministry if you feel that's unfair. You are not qualified. You are asking for trouble if you intend to be in the ministry. Once you accept the call of God on your life, you must accept this matter as a "given"—that people will always view you differently.

I was called into the ministry when I was nineteen years old. Three months later I was called to be the pastor of the Church of the Nazarene in Palmer, Tennessee. I was startled to realize that these people were actually taking me seriously! I rather thought they might say, "Oh, isn't he sweet," and overlook my youth and inexperience. But no. I was their pastor. They listened to what I said—in and out of the pulpit. I fear I failed many times in this area. God was gracious and patient with me. And so were some of them. But not all. One year later when "recall" time came, I scraped through with one vote enough to stay on. But I soon resigned; I was not ready for that—then.

2. God requires more of you.

But what is far more serious is the fact that God Himself judges us more strictly. He clamps down on us in areas where He is not so hard with others. This may not bless you, but He seems to let the people of God generally get away with more than we in the ministry can get away with. Unfair? Sorry about that—but that's the way it is. He may give them—to use an expression every golfer understands—a handicap. But not us!

God disciplines more strictly, judges more harshly, observes more carefully, and scrutinizes more often all those who accept His call to enter into the teaching or preaching ministry. This is what He does here below, and says nothing about being judged at the judgment seat of Christ. We who are in the ministry are being dealt with here below day and night—all the time—on this earth. But when we stand before God at the final judgment, we will find that there, too, we will be judged more strictly. To put it another way, it will be somewhat harder for us to get a reward at the judgment seat of Christ than for those not in the ministry.

This should sober anybody who is thinking about going into the ministry. If you are not called by the Holy Spirit, you really are asking for trouble if you pursue the ministry. Stay away from it!

Chapter Fourteen

THE PROOF OF SELF-CONTROL

If anyone can control his tongue, it proves that he has perfect control over himself in every other way.

—JAMES 3:2, TLB

A FRUIT OF THE SPIRIT IS "SELF-CONTROL," along with love, joy, peace, patience, and other virtues. Self-control sometimes gets lost in this list of the fruit of the Spirit. When you stop and think about it, it is an extraordinary virtue. Surely one of the primary things that separate a Christian from a non-Christian is that we have self-control. We are not mastered by any sin!

But what is the proof that we have this self-control? Is it because we are not addicted to alcohol, tobacco, sex, pornography, drugs, or excessive eating? Some may say that our not being a slave to these proves that we have self-control. This is true—up to a point. But according to James, the proof of self-control is that we control our tongues.

The Greek literally reads, as in the King James Version, "If any offend not in word, the same is a perfect man, and able to bridle the whole body." The offense in word does not refer to sound or perfect doctrine, although we should aspire to this. James is talking about overcoming a loose tongue, unguarded and needlessly offensive comments. By "whole body" he is not saying that tongue control will heal the body; he is talking about "every other part of his personality" (PHILLIPS).

The truth is, James did not introduce the subject of the tongue in James 3, but early on in this wonderful epistle. For example, the first impulse we often have when we are tempted is to say, "I am tempted of God," or "God is tempting me." One must begin control of the tongue in the presence of God—and never accuse the Lord of tempting us, because "God cannot be tempted by evil, nor does he tempt anyone" (James 1:13). Strength of character is refusing to say what you might think or feel, when you know in your heart that saying it will make things worse. Hence James gave that famous axiom: "Everyone should be quick to listen, slow to speak and slow to become angry" (v. 19).

The tongue is the indicator of the heart: "Out of the abundance of the heart the mouth speaks" (Matt. 12:34, NKJV). But you may reply, "Then one automatically says what is on his heart—if you think it, do it." Wrong. That is the devil speaking. What is on your heart may be right and good; it could be very wrong and evil. Tongue control is to discern your heart with objectivity so that you do not say what the devil would have you say.

There is a difference between temptation and sin. It is not a sin to be tempted; it is not a sin to have the thought. The sin is in our *words*—when we say what is tempting us. The temptation could be to lust or self-exaltation, name dropping, or speaking ungraciously. The temptation to say such things is not sin; it is sin when we cave in to the temptation to cause another to lust, to say what makes us look good, or to say what will make another look bad. Tongue control indicates whether the temptation was aborted and sin did not come forth.

The tongue, therefore, proves whether you are in control of your whole being. That is the fruit of the Spirit—self-control. The perfect man or woman, therefore, is not the one who doesn't have evil thoughts or wrong feelings; perfection is buttoning your lip so you do not say what you feel like saying. When we say what we feel in such circumstances, it makes things worse. This is why James says that the tongue is a "small spark" that becomes a fire that can spread and do unthinkable damage (James 3:5–6).

The perfect man or woman is the one who can "bridle" his or her entire personality. The tongue, therefore, is not seen by James in these lines as a positive thing but negative. The tongue has no ability to come up with the right answer, no gift automatically to produce fruit. The function of the tongue in the Christian life is to abort temptation by refusing to speak. James is suggesting to us that if we will take care of the negative—by bridling the tongue—God will take care of the positive—speaking as the Holy Spirit would have us do.

James continues, "When we put bits into the mouths of horses to make them obey us, we can turn the whole animal"

(James 3:3). As O. S. Hawkins says, "No horse has ever bridled himself. Its master must do that. Likewise, try as we may, we cannot bridle ourselves. We need to yield our speech to the Master's control in order to receive direction in life. The bridle under a master's control benefits the horse by making him productive and leading him down the right path. Similarly, allowing the Master to control our tongues is for our own good."[1]

DOES THE GIFT OF TONGUES BRING TONGUE CONTROL?

I want to talk about tongues—the gift of tongues. Some sectors of the church emphasize the fruit of the Spirit to the neglect of the gifts; other movements of the church stress the gifts of the Spirit to the neglect of the fruit of the Spirit. To those who speak in tongues, one wants to ask: does speaking in tongues help you control your tongue? If speaking in tongues brought tongue control, it would be a tremendous testimony to the gift of tongues. But to my knowledge, alas, there does not seem to be a great correlation between speaking in tongues and controlling the tongue. I don't mean to be unfair, but I fear there are those who are intense about *speaking* in tongues who have not developed *control* of their tongues—that is, speaking in love and never pointing the finger or giving in to gossip.

This is not to be hard on those who speak in tongues. I speak in tongues. But I have to confess that speaking in tongues so far (I have been doing it for many years) has not given me great conscious help in tongue control. I find that my gift of tongues sometimes works without the fruit of the Spirit manifesting simultaneously. This is because the gifts are without repentance—that is, they are irrevocable (Rom. 11:29). This means that speaking in tongues is no sign of true spirituality. As a matter of fact, you can have the gifts of the Spirit and not be a spiritual person. King Saul prophesied (one of the gifts of the Spirit—see 1 Corinthians 12:8–10) while he was on his way to kill David (1 Sam. 19:18–24).

What is even sadder is that there are those who emphasize the gift of tongues so much that they tend to judge people who do not speak in tongues as being less spiritual. Indeed, there are those who stress speaking in tongues with such vigor that they sometimes seem more anxious to get people to speak in tongues than they care about saving the lost. They become "evangelistic" regarding the gift of tongues—and get heated up sometimes when people disagree with them.

I say this lovingly as I know people who speak in tongues but do not seem to have tongue control. It is not a good testimony for the gifts of the Spirit when we are deficient in the fruit of the Spirit. And one of the fruit of the Spirit is self-control! According to James, you do not have genuine self-control until you are able to control the tongue. It is the fruit of the Spirit that is relevant here. If we want the gifts of the Spirit to be enticing to those who are scared of them, we should hang our heads in shame if we do not have the fruit of the Spirit.

I take the view that there has been a silent divorce in the church, speaking generally, between the Word and the Spirit. When there is a divorce, sometimes the children stay with the mother, sometimes with the father. In this divorce between the Word and the Spirit, there are those on the "Word" side and those on the "Spirit" side. Word people emphasize doctrine, expository preaching, and upholding the faith once delivered to the church—and, yes, the *fruit* of the Spirit. Spirit people emphasize signs, wonders, miracles, and the need to return to the Book of Acts—and, yes, the *gifts* of the Spirit.

What is needed today more than anything is not one or the other but both! I personally suspect that the simultaneous combination would result in spontaneous combustion.

But any emphasis on the gifts without the fruit of the Spirit will be an unbalanced treatment of the New Testament and a gross example of being selective with God's infallible Word. Therefore speaking in tongues—the only gift of the Spirit that challenges our pride and therefore has the potential to keep one humble—will not be very attractive to those who try so hard to pursue the fruit of the Spirit, including control of the tongue. If we want people to desire our gifts, then we are duty bound to manifest self-control.

According to James, the effort to control the tongue is the place to begin. But we will see that we have our work cut out for us!

Chapter Fifteen

THE DANGEROUS POTENTIAL OF THE TONGUE

Consider what a great forest is set on fire by a small spark. The tongue also is a fire, a world of evil among the parts of the body.

—JAMES 3:5–6

The tongue has the power of life and death.

—PROVERBS 18:21

THE TONGUE IS A MOST EXTRAORDINARY PART of the body. By it we speak, send signals, feel, and taste. It is unimaginable what life would be without the tongue. I think of people who are not able to speak; what an inconvenience to lose the privilege of speaking or to be born without speech. Zechariah, the father of John the Baptist, was unable to speak for a period of time (Luke 1:20, 64). This was a temporary judgment inflicted upon him by the Spirit of God owing to his unbelief. How horrible it must have been for him in those days. And yet to live like this all the time is to experience much frustration.

The tongue is an instrument for incalculable good. By the tongue, we praise God and sing to His glory: "His praise was on my tongue" (Ps. 66:17). "My tongue will tell of your righteous acts all day long" (Ps. 71:24). "May my tongue sing of your word, for all your commands are righteous" (Ps. 119:172). "Our mouths were filled with laughter, our tongues with songs of joy" (Ps. 126:2). By the tongue we spread the Word of God: "My tongue will speak of your righteousness" (Ps. 35:28). The tongue is the instrument of good teaching: "My tongue is the pen of a skillful writer" (Ps. 45:1). "The Sovereign LORD has given me an instructed tongue, to know the word that sustains the weary" (Isa. 50:4). It is the tongue that will one day proclaim the glory of Jesus Christ throughout the universe, because "every tongue [shall] confess that Jesus Christ is Lord, to the glory of God the Father" (Phil. 2:11).

But did you know how little "good" the tongue is actually said to do when you check the references to it in the Bible? I was amazed. The word *tongue* is found in the Bible no fewer than 130 times. Except where it means language, the word *tongue* is seen as largely negative or potentially damaging in most places. I had to search diligently to get the positive quotations above! But consider, for example, these typical words:

You will be protected from the lash of the tongue.

—JOB 5:21

With their tongue they speak deceit.

—PSALM 5:9

Trouble and evil are under his tongue.

—PSALM 10:7

Keep your tongue from evil.

—PSALM 34:13

I will watch my ways and keep my tongue from sin.

—PSALM 39:1

Your tongue plots destruction; it is like a sharpened razor.

—PSALM 52:2

A lying tongue hates those it hurts.

—PROVERBS 26:28

These are but a few verses, and I did not include the many references to "mouth," "word," "words," or "lips" where you read equivalent descriptions that are mostly negative.

Yes, the potential for good is unlimited: "A word aptly spoken is like apples of gold in settings of silver" (Prov. 25:11). Indeed, a word that is uttered even with no emotion or much volume can accomplish what no one had dreamed, as when a "gentle tongue can break a bone" (v. 15). I watched with amazement when a cabinet minister in the British Parliament in one stroke brought down the career of former prime minister Margaret Thatcher in a few moments with a calm voice.

A famous anecdote reveals how the boisterous and unprepared preacher had written to the side of his notes: "weak point, shout here." There are times when raising the voice is good and right, as when Peter preached to thousands on the Day of Pentecost (Acts 2:14). But if one shouts and harangues with no substantial content, the speaker is like a mouth full of gravel, with the result being an audience with empty heads and hearts.

"NO MAN CAN TAME THE TONGUE"

James points out that we can in some ways get the advantage over nature or creation. For example, we make a horse obey us with a bridle. We can work with the wind and direct a ship's direction by a small rudder (James 3:3–4). He then shows the damage the tongue—such a small member of the body—can do. We might expect him to say what we can do to get on top of things when it comes to tongue control. But he concludes that the tongue "no man can tame" (v. 8). Nobody can. Not a single person under heaven. Old or young. Rich or poor. No matter one's color, race, or nationality. Tongue control cannot be attained by any gift we have, by any amount of education we receive, or by the highest level of intellect. (Now that would be unfair—giving smarter people an advantage!) But a high IQ doesn't even help. More involvement in Christian service will not bring you one whit closer to tongue control. Mixing with the elite, being upwardly mobile, making more money—all these are of no value in achieving control of the tongue.

And now for what may seem very astonishing to you (I wish it weren't so), James does not even say that there is anything that *God* promises to do for us if we meet certain conditions. You read correctly: not even God Himself promises to step in and give us relief in connection with tongue control. There are no simple promises that "if we do *this*, God will do *that*." Not so with becoming a Christian. To attain salvation, all we have to do is to meet a simple condition: believe on the Lord Jesus Christ, and we will be saved. The Bible is full of promises, offered on the basis of meeting certain conditions.

James does not offer one single promise that, if we meet a certain condition, God will fix the tongue. Now he did so regarding the promise of wisdom. He said that if we lack wisdom, we should ask God for it—in faith. Faith without wavering meets the condition for getting wisdom (James 1:5–6). Moreover, we are promised the crown of life if we persevere when tried (v. 12). He said later on in his letter that if we resist the devil (a condition), he will flee from us (the promise) (James 4:7). He added that if you meet the condition of drawing close to God, God promises that "he will come near to you" (v. 8). So we know, therefore, that James promises a lot of good things in his mighty little epistle—attaching certain conditions, using or implying the word *if*.

But he does not offer a single promise of tongue control if we do certain things. If only he had said, "Pray more, and you will achieve tongue control." I wish he had said, "Read your Bible every day, and you will master the tongue." I would even welcome the challenge from him, "Go on a forty-day fast, and you will conquer your tongue."

A colorful, widely used, and powerful preacher in the Church of the Nazarene known as Uncle Buddy Robinson was speaking in my old church and gave an altar call for people to come forward. A lady was kneeling and praying at the altar and apparently getting nowhere. Uncle Buddy asked, "What is your problem?" She replied, "I can't get my tongue on the altar." Uncle Buddy said to her, "Sister, I can't see what the problem is. Your tongue is only four inches long and this altar is thirty feet long—surely you can get your tongue on it." Quite. If only.

TAKE RESPONSIBILITY FOR YOUR WORDS

One of James's very purposes and motives in these lines is to bring us to the place that we see there is no hope of bridling the tongue—if we are expecting God to do it. Indeed, he wants us to see that there is no hope of taming the tongue until we accept that God *isn't going to do it* for us. Why? It is because as long as we think that God will somehow take over, we won't do the first thing about it!

Take the matter of lust, which is treated earlier in this epistle (James 1:13–15). If you think that God is behind your being tempted, you will somehow expect Him, not you, to be the one to eradicate or control that lust. You conclude, therefore, that you are not responsible for your lust—He is. Wrong. We all have to deal with our own lust—and never accuse God. Each of us is tempted when we are enticed by our *own* evil desire. We are complete fools if we don't deal with it.

James elaborates on the danger of the uncontrolled tongue in these lines (James 3:3–8). When it comes to lust, he shows that the end is death if the process of being tempted is not aborted along the way (James 1:15). When it comes to the tongue, he shows the potential damage that can come from it when it is not controlled. The tongue is "a small part of the body"—a fact everybody knows. But even a Christian can do great damage, he warns us, if the tongue is not controlled. Conversion did not conquer the tongue problem. There is not a promised work of grace—second, third, fourth, tenth, or hundredth—that will root out the problem of the tongue.

As a forest fire is started by a small spark, the tongue "also is a fire" and spreads evil to all parts of the body—and we could add, the body of Christ. It corrupts the "whole person," but equally spreads rapidly through the people of God and causes disruption, disunity, degradation, defeat, and despair. It happens in families, at work, or wherever we are in the world.

What is James's point if there is nothing we can do and there is nothing that God promises to do? Is he trying to demoralize us? No. It is a wake-up call to take responsibility for our words and deeds so that we will be consciously aware and able to improve. God made us in such a way that we do change by being warned and seeing the consequences. We do! We are more likely to change when we see the danger and results if we don't change.

So does this mean that we can control the tongue after all? I answer: when we are sufficiently warned and motivated, we will take care not to grieve the Holy Spirit of God and will make changes. It does not mean we will be perfect. But we can still improve. It is with the help of God and our working at it. In the words of Oliver Cromwell, "Trust God and keep your powder dry." It is a cooperative effort that effects change and can stop us from disaster.

WILL GOD TAME THE TONGUE?

Some may wish to say, "Man can't tame the tongue, but God can." Yes. He can indeed. But He probably won't. God can do a lot of things. He can stop hurricanes. He can stop earthquakes. He can stop crime. I used to say at Westminster Chapel, "Boys and girls, God can do your homework for you." But He never did mine! God motivates us by a strong word of warning. We are so stupid to ignore His Word. When sufficiently motivated, we will begin to take care when it comes to our words. We will likely start dealing with the tongue when we realize God won't do it for us—or when we have been vehemently awakened. Probably not before. This is what James is trying to do for us, however.

I used to prepare sermons in a certain hotel in central London. I had a place where I could be alone, where nobody knew me and only my wife knew where I was. One day when I went to park outside the hotel, I noticed a huge "X" marking the spot where I was going to park. It extended the length of the car. Someone said the parking place was marked for diplomatic use only. I questioned that and parked there anyway. When I came out a few hours later, my car was missing. I rushed into the hotel to report my stolen car. But when asked where I had parked it, the manager pointed out that that space was for a diplomat and that I might try calling the police to see where my car was. I did. They had it. They had towed it to North London—an hour's drive away—where I headed with the help of an expensive taxi ride. I had to pay a fee to retrieve the car and then received a huge penalty fine in the mail a few weeks later. I can say one thing: it worked! I never parked there again. Was it God who helped me? Perhaps. Or was I sufficiently motivated not to park there? Yes.

That is the way the mind of James works in these verses. Not that controlling the tongue is as easy as avoiding an illegal parking place. But there are things we can and must do if we are to improve on tongue control. We will not get to perfection. Sorry about that! But we can improve. The paradox of Christian perfection is to admit our imperfection but strive for perfection nonetheless. God likes that. It works. We can get better. Not perfect. Better.

Chapter Sixteen

THE FIRE OF HELL

The tongue also is a fire... and is itself set on fire by hell.

—JAMES 3:6

The Lord disciplines those he loves.

—HEBREWS 12:6

IN HIS EPISTLE, JAMES IS DOING HIS BEST TO GIVE every Christian a wake-up call. I call it internal chastening—warning of serious consequences through the Word. There are three levels of chastening, or disciplining:

1. Internal

2. External

3. Terminal

INTERNAL CHASTENING

The word translated "chasten" (KJV) or "discipline" (NIV) comes from the Greek *paideuo*—a word that means "enforced learning." It is when God teaches us a lesson in such a way that we are without excuse if we remain the same afterwards.

To put it another way, internal chastening is God's Plan A for securing our obedience to His Word. Plan A comes through teaching, preaching, worshiping, fellowship, a slap on the wrist from a friend, or wise counseling. Whenever God speaks to us without putting us flat on our backs to get our attention, we should welcome it. Plan A is the best way to get our problems solved. This happens when we hear Him speak and we reply, "Yes, Lord"—and also prove it by a life of more careful obedience.

EXTERNAL CHASTENING

Then there is Plan B—external chastening. It is when God uses external force rather than the Word. He may indeed put us on our backs. He may bring sickness, financial reverse, loss, exposure, the withholding of vindication, marriage breakdown, or any number of things. It is when Plan A fails that God institutes Plan B to get our attention. It too is a wake-up call, but it is more painful. It is carried out by a loving heavenly Father because we did not listen to Him when He was carrying out Plan A.

The Epistle of James is Plan A. But in James 3:5–7, James *describes* what I am calling Plan B. He lets us see how bad it can get if we don't listen to his warning to deal with the tongue. He shows the horror that the unguarded comment can cause, what pointing the finger will do, what spreading gossip leads to, what sending people on a guilt trip ends up doing, or what accusing God brings on. God steps in with Plan B because we did not take heed to the Word.

God's Plan B can be pretty awful. Things happen that are so dreadful—it is called the fire of hell—that we would give a thousand worlds to turn the clock back so we could listen one more time to Plan A.

TERMINAL CHASTENING

Plan C is carried out by God when even Plan B fails. It is the worst possible scenario for a true Christian. This is evidenced when either a person cannot be renewed again to repentance (Heb. 6:6) or when one commits the sin unto death (Acts 5:1–10; 1 Cor. 11:30; 1 John 5:16). If God bringing on external chastening doesn't wake us up so as truly to get our attention, we leave God with no choice but to judge us with terminal chastening—the final measure of disciplining. I have developed this more fully in *The Judgment Seat of Christ.*[1]

The saddest thing in the world in this matter is that you cannot take back what you have said. The careless word was a spark that started a forest fire. We may say "I'm sorry" and mean it, but the damage has already been done: "An offended brother is more unyielding than a fortified city" (Prov. 18:19). We may cry out, "I wish to God I hadn't said it," but it is too late. The spark started the fire. All the water from the seven seas would not put out the fire.

In a courtroom, a defense lawyer or prosecutor may lead a witness to say something that the judge overrules. The judge orders it stricken from the record and cautions the jury to disregard the comment. But everybody knows it was said, and many don't forget it when they deliberate for a verdict. The overruled word often still rules and reigns.

I have known occasions when God mercifully, if not miraculously, stopped me from uttering something that would have been disastrous. I have also known occasions when Matthew 10:20 (about taking no thought of what to say but letting the Holy Spirit speak through you) was in operation. Yes, sometimes in what I can only call an "emergency situation," God may reach down and stop our mouths or control our tongues.

HEED THE WARNING

But the Christian life is to be lived generally in nonemergency conditions. We must not expect Him to treat us as if we were in a life-and-death situation all the time, constantly rescuing us from ourselves and giving us perfect words. God does not work with us apart from the real world we live in. The sooner we accept this, the sooner it will have an effect on the way we speak. James wanted to help us avoid tragedies.

I don't know anybody who can read this section of James and feel good. It is disquieting, discomforting, and sobering. If reading this does that for you—good. There is hope.

James wanted to box us in. If we get defensive, however, we will not learn a thing from him. And yet it is far better to get angry with him—and still later take his warning on board—than to say, "Yes, Lord," and not change. Jesus's parable of the two sons is appropriate here:

> There was a man who had two sons. He went to the first and said, "Son, go and work today in the vineyard." "I will not," he answered, but later he changed his mind and went. Then the father went to the other son and said the same thing. He answered, "I will, sir," but he did not go. Which of the two did what his father wanted? "The first," they answered.
>
> —MATTHEW 21:28–31

In a word, if reading this book brings an immediate "Yes, Lord," that is good—so far. But the worst thing that can happen is to be instantly and immediately stirred—then revert to your old ways. I would far prefer that you say no and be upset, except that you are shortly granted repentance so you can be renewed again. This shows that Plan B is working and that you have not fallen into terminal chastening.

James's goal for us is that we—in ever-increasing measure—will experience the wisdom that comes from heaven that is "first of all pure; then peace-loving, considerate, submissive, full of mercy and good fruit, impartial and sincere" (James 3:17). We get closer and closer to this goal by taking his words with utmost seriousness.

DON'T GIVE SATAN THE PLEASURE

"A fool gives full vent to anger, but a wise person quietly holds it back" (Prov. 29:11, NLT). Giving full vent to your anger is when the devil achieves his wish for you—that you lose your temper, shout, and blame—and leave all around you scared and upset. That is when the fire of hell sweeps through your life and surroundings. The devil has a party in hell, as it were, drinking to his victory over you and to your defeat in controlling the tongue. My loving advice: *don't give Satan that pleasure.*

To be honest with you, if there has been some improvement in me over the years, it has been because God carried out Plan B in my life—more often than I want you to know. I know what it is to set a forest on fire by my uncontrolled words—to feel the very fire of hell when the breath of Satan entered the room and won a big victory.

It is not a happy thought that the devil got in and orchestrated our words. But this has happened to me, and it can happen to you. When all hell breaks loose through our tongues, it is because the tongue was set on fire by hell itself. The tongue is a fire that spreads evil throughout our entire personality. We lose control. We say things that would make the angels blush. We would die a thousand deaths if a video of ourselves would be replayed before the world. It all happened because the devil entered in—through a spark—and won. Like a pilot light in a stove or an oven waiting to be ignited by gas, so the tongue just needs a spark to burst into flames.

The tongue, therefore, can be inflamed by hell. The tongue is not only what made hell necessary; hell itself ultimately lies behind tongues that spread deadly poison. It is the behind-the-scenes explanation for anger, lost tempers, contorted faces, wounded feelings, and words that engender jealousy and fear. It is all because the tongue is itself set on fire by hell (the Greek word *gehenna* is the word actually used). *Gehenna* (used twelve times) is the principle word used in the New Testament for hell. *Gehenna* was the place where rubbish was burnt outside one of the city gates of Jerusalem. The fires of *gehenna* were always burning.

Jesus adopted this word *gehenna* for His teaching of everlasting punishment. And James uses it to connote the idea that Satan's future and final place of destiny, which exists now, somehow works its way into conversations when we are not sufficiently careful.

Why is the tongue called fire? Because it gets so easily out of control. Whatever it burns is destroyed and brought to complete disuse; what is burnt is never the same again. It is called fire because what we do to ourselves is damaged, sometimes taking a good while to get things back together. The tongue is a ready and most cooperative weapon when the urge to speak—to "put the record straight" or to have the last word—takes over. It is called fire because we so often do irreparable damage to others—even those closest to us.

Satan knows all about hell. It is the fire of hell that motivates the devil to work so violently. He knows where he is going to end up. He knows his time is short (Rev. 12:12). It is his knowledge of his impending doom that lies behind the violence that he does.

He knows he is going to hell. The tongue is his best weapon to conserve the damage already done, and it is his best weapon to continue the spread of evil.

In a word, the devil is on the road to hell and wants to take as many with him as possible. He wants to create chaos in the meantime. He wants to inflame and paralyze Christians. He wants Christians to get burned by their words. He wants Christians to burn others by an ill choice of words. It happens in families. In marriages. In church meetings and business meetings. In deacons' meetings. In parking lots after the church service. In cars on the way to church.

> It [the tongue] represents among our members the world with
> all its wickedness; it pollutes our whole being; it keeps the
> wheel of our existence red-hot, and its flames are fed by hell.
>
> —James 3:6, neb

Hell was created for the devil and his angels (Matt. 25:41). Satan fell by uttering threatening words such as, "I will be like God" (Isa. 14:14). The tongue brought about his own downfall. He has been seeking vengeance ever since by getting people to do what he did—and utter heinous and, if possible, blasphemous words. He wants to bring about our downfall and destroy all he can before he meets his own final doom. His anger toward God, his hatred toward righteousness, his ire toward every child of God, and his wrath toward all that is good are so quickly displayed once we lose tongue control.

THERE IS HOPE FOR THE TONGUE

Poisonous words corrupt our whole person, says James. We are left demoralized, weakened, compromised, defeated, and jaundiced. All is yellow to the jaundiced eye. We are angry with the world. Our loved ones. Our friends. Our neighbors. Ourselves. The Dove—the Holy Spirit—lifts from us and flies away, leaving us to ourselves. We become unteachable. Defensive. Irritable. Full of self-pity. Full of unkindness. When we speak in that condition, nothing comes out right.

This means sometimes that we are seriously backslidden. It does not mean that Plan C is the next thing God is going to put into operation. That would only happen if one does not wake up. Not waking up after so many forms of external chastenings—and seeing the fire of hell manifested before our eyes—is certainly not a good sign. But as long as you can feel truly remorseful and repentant, there is hope.

The proof that we are not in a terminal-chastening mode is that we are given sorrow for sin. God grants unfeigned repentance. We confess it to Him. When we do so, He is faithful and just to forgive us our sins and to cleanse us from all unrighteousness (1 John 1:9). Not only are we granted the ability to repent, but we are also changed from glory to glory by the Holy Spirit (2 Cor. 3:18). As long as we enjoy being changed from glory to glory, it is a wonderful sign that not only have we not become stone-deaf to the Spirit, but also that God is at work in us. Knowing this is a very good feeling.

Repentance (in the Greek, *metanoia*—"change of mind") shows that we are still being changed. Despite our stupidity and folly, God stoops to our weakness to give us help. It shows He is not finished with us. The worst scenario, then, is to become stone-deaf to the Spirit—that we hear nothing from Him. But if the Word of God convicts us, it means we are not stone-deaf to His Spirit but are indeed hearing His voice. Wonderful feeling, indeed.

So do not be discouraged if you have failed with the tongue. Do not be demoralized if you have flamed the fires of hell. Do not be in despair just because the devil celebrated a victory over you.

Why? Because the devil always overreaches himself. If you will stand on God's Word when you are put through the fire, you will see—in time—that what happened that was bad will still work together for good (Rom. 8:28).

> When through fiery trials thy pathway shall lie,
> My grace, all sufficient, shall be thy supply.
> The flames shall not hurt thee; I only design
> Thy dross to consume and thy gold to refine.[2]
>
> —George Keith

I believe I should tell you that I think I have made nearly every mistake that could be made when it comes to lack of tongue control. But God has been patient with me. Our heavenly Father is a gracious God. I ought to know.

Chapter Seventeen

POISON

No man can tame the tongue. It is a restless evil, full of deadly poison.

—JAMES 3:8

THE TONGUE IS NOT A NEUTRAL THING. IT IS A vile part of our being and is—in and of itself—intrinsically evil, wicked, and poisonous. It is not our words that make the tongue deadly poisonous; the tongue is already poisonous before we utter a single word. This is because the tongue mirrors the heart. Jesus said, "Out of the heart come evil thoughts, murder, adultery, sexual immorality, theft, false testimony, slander" (Matt. 15:19). This is Jesus's diagnosis of the heart of all men and women. These startling words to the self-righteous Pharisees followed His statement that "the things that come *out of the mouth* come from the heart" (v. 18, emphasis added).

Now you know where James got his teaching.

James contrasts the tongue with nature: "All kinds of animals, birds, reptiles and creatures of the sea are being tamed and have been tamed by man, but no man can tame the tongue" (James 3:7–8). Such living creatures are not guilty of deadly, poisonous tongues.

Does this surprise you? Did you think that the tongue of a human being is a neutral member of our personality? Natural, yes, but not neutral.

Behind all that James teaches us—which he got straight from Jesus—is his robust doctrine of sin. We may not like it. We have seen the importance of a biblical doctrine of sin already in the book you are reading. It is a matter so often swept under the carpet. We are living in a day when the church, speaking generally, has such a superficial doctrine of sin that we should not be surprised at our lack of impact in the world. First, many have forgotten that we are *born* with a fallen nature. Second, many have also forgotten that we *retain* this fallen nature after conversion—and will have it until we see Jesus face-to-face (1 John 3:2). That is what theologians call glorification (Rom. 8:30).

It seems almost redundant to say it, but we are not glorified yet. We are still sinners. To recall Martin Luther's coined phrase, "simultaneous saint and sinner"—referring to every Christian, the holiest man or woman is still a sinner. This may not fare well with some people's doctrine of sanctification, but this is what Jesus taught, it is what the apostle Paul taught, and it is what James is telling us in these lines that are quite out of our comfort zone.

A SOBER DOCTRINE OF SIN

The tongue, he tells us, *is* (not was) "a restless evil, full of deadly poison." Furthermore, it does not become that; it *is* that. James is describing your tongue and mine. He is describing his own tongue. The apostle John's tongue. Peter's tongue. Elijah's tongue. Daniel's tongue. Abraham's tongue. Moses's tongue. King David's tongue. Only Jesus was born without sin, and only Jesus lived without ever sinning (Heb. 4:15).

I was brought up to believe in "sinless perfection"—or something very close to that. I was taught that a Christian does not sin because a Christian must live above sin. As for James's comment "we all stumble in many ways," they would say that stumbling is not necessarily sinning. They would call it "mistake," "error," "fault," or anything other than *sin*. When I used to ask why Jesus gave us the Lord's Prayer that includes "forgive us our trespasses" (sins) if He knew Christians could reach a state of grace that puts one beyond daily sinning, some would say that the prayer was given "before Pentecost"—or give no answer at all.

Even if you do not have my background, I ask you: do you have a good understanding of sin, of the human heart, of what is true of all people?

My ministry over the past fifty years has crossed many denominational and theological lines. I have been blessed in this regard. I have been fortunate to minister to people of many different theological, cultural, ethnic, and church backgrounds. It is my observation that most Christians have a deficient doctrine of sin. A superficial understanding of sin will mean a shallow theology. J. I. Packer says that the Bible Belt is a thousand miles wide and one inch deep.

We are simply not happy to think that we are wicked inside. We like to think that our being saved—or being filled with the Spirit—moves us beyond having to see ourselves as "vile," to use Augustus Toplady's word in his classic hymn "Rock of Ages."

Why is this so important? I answer: that we will not be shocked at ourselves when poison proceeds from our mouths. It is important to our sanity, our peace, and our understanding of God and His Word. Do not be surprised if you discover that the degree to which you come to terms with the wickedness of your tongue and its potential for danger will be the degree to which you are motivated to control that tongue.

Holiness is achieved, little by little, not in proportion to our denying sin but in proportion to our coming to terms with its existence—in ourselves. "If we claim to be without sin, we deceive ourselves and the truth is not in us" (1 John 1:8). These words should shake us rigid as James's word about our tongues being restless evils and full of deadly poison should do. James and John have the same doctrine of sin.

DO NOT DESPISE RUGGED SELF-DISCIPLINE

James does not write these words as if to say, "Get rid of this condition; do something about it." He does not pose a work of grace that will bring the tongue back to the pre-fallen state of human beings. The vile tongues we are born with are here to stay—that is, as long as we are in this world.

If there were a work of grace that would enable one to put his or her tongue on the altar and then be totally delivered, *ah*—how nice and lovely!

Some want to deal with the problem through casting out demons—by exorcisms. If only. I wish. I have had some very sincere Charismatic friends try to cast demons out of me—more than once. I can tell you, I want all the help I can get, and I will go anywhere to get the final victory over the tongue in advance of glory. The problem is, I happened to notice (do forgive me for this) that those who wanted to cast out demons must have had demons themselves because they too had problems with tongue control, temper, pointing the finger, gossip, and, in some cases, lust. Oh, dear.

Don't get me wrong. I believe there are demons. I also believe in deliverance from demons. But not all problems are demonic. Making demons the explanation for all our maladies is often a cop-out in order to avoid rugged self-discipline.

We are better off to believe James—and accept what he says about the tongue. It is not a neutral member of the body. It mirrors the heart. The heart is the fountain of all the evil speaking we do.

Thank God for the blood of Jesus. As we walk in the light as He is in the light, we have fellowship with Him, and His blood cleanses us from all sin (1 John 1:7). The cleansing is not eradicating sin or pulling it out by the roots; it is making us feel forgiven, giving us peace, and enabling us to face our heavenly Father knowing He knows all about us and still loves us! The cleansing of the blood of Jesus is what gives us intimacy with the Father, joy in the Holy Spirit, and the feeling of being totally forgiven. It comes as we walk in the light.

Part of walking in that light is accepting what James says about the tongue and then being sufficiently convicted that we want to do something about it. We can. There is more that we can do than we may want to admit to.

Some people go from one extreme to the other. On the one hand they want to say that the tongue is a neutral thing—as if to say that we do not stumble in many ways. The other extreme is to say that God will control the tongue for us if we let Him!

James adopts neither view. The truth lies between both extremes. Our tongues are deadly poison; we can still improve and aim for perfection. The burden is on us to fight this battle, to get better and better at overcoming unguarded comments, and to stop engaging in pointing the finger. We can all do more than we may want to concede.

The tongue is, therefore, not a neutral thing but is by nature leaning toward hell's pull. It waits for our lack of self-control to ignite the flame or spread its poison in order to give the devil a victory.

THE TONGUE AND OUR FALLEN NATURE

The tongue is the official spokesman for our fallen nature. Biblical theology teaches us that there is fallen nature (people) and unfallen nature (trees and animals). Although nature is affected by the Fall, it is not properly said to be fallen. Nature is cursed due to the Fall (Gen. 3:17), but there is nothing sinful about nature.

"All kinds of animals, birds, reptiles and creatures of the sea are being tamed and have been tamed by man" (James 3:7). It is man—woman—who is the culprit. The tongue is the immediate indicator of our motivation: our sexual urge, self-esteem, and ambition.

The easiest and most natural thing in the world is to give in to the heart, whether it be jealousy, sexual temptation, saying something unflattering about another, accusing and blaming people, or giving in to bitterness or fear. Lust is inflamed by the tongue. Jealousy increases by the tongue. Our defensiveness gets worse when the tongue gets involved. You try to get the last word, and you lose control.

You say to yourself, "I will feel better if I get this off my chest." So you do it. You get it off your chest. Lo and behold, you *do* feel better. For a while. But only for a while. The poison you spouted did not rid the heart of that poison; it only let it settle for a short time. Like pornography, which plays into an insatiable appetite for lust, so the tongue saying what it feels like saying only lets the poison build up until the volcano erupts next time. "The heart is deceitful above all things and beyond cure" (Jer. 17:9).

Our heart is an incurable part of fallen nature, says James. All else in nature is tamable: animals, fish, reptiles, birds. Man was given dominion over all creatures—animals, birds, fish (Gen. 1:26, 28). The devil isn't interested in getting at beasts, fish, or birds. A bird, fish, or tree can't spread evil! Satan's natural enemy is man—all because we were created in God's image (Gen. 1:26). Satan hates *us*—not flowers, mountains, giraffes, groupers, dolphins, monkeys, dogs, cats, or birds. Satan's archenemy is the

Lord Jesus Christ. Satan hates Jesus because He did not take on the nature of angels but the nature of mankind—the seed of Abraham (Heb. 2:16, KJV). God was made *flesh* (John 1:14). That's us! All that Satan can do to man is an attack on Jesus Christ.

To put it another way: Satan is jealous of us. He cannot be redeemed. But we can. He cannot be saved. But we can. He cannot improve. But we can. He hates the Savior of the world who came to save people. The devil is jealous of Jesus Christ; therefore, he hates us who are His brothers and sisters (Heb. 2:11).

What Satan feels toward us is best expressed with the word *poison*—deadly poison. Poison destroys. So in order to inflict injury on the body of Jesus Christ, the devil appeals to our fallen nature to say poisonous things—to make others feel bad and look bad. He himself already feels that way, but he cannot get that across without our help. Our poisonous tongues oblige.

Do you realize what a high privilege it is to be made in the image of God? Satan hates us because we resemble God. Do you realize what a wonderful privilege it is to be called sons of God? The devil hates us because we resemble Jesus Christ. Do you realize what an honor it is for us to participate in the cosmic war between Christ and Satan? We will one day participate in his everlasting downfall. He knows that and hates us for it. But we will be praising God throughout eternity for this privilege.

Thus, to the extent that we learn to be slow in speaking and quick in listening, we will be less likely to manifest wrath. I say to you and to myself: let us not give the devil an inch. Let us beware that our poisonous tongues are vulnerable and overly willing to cooperate with his evil suggestions—especially if we have an enemy, if we have been deeply hurt by somebody, or if we are jealous of another. The devil has a computer printout on our personalities, strengths, weaknesses, hurts, liabilities, enemies, and friends. He is extremely clever. My dad used to say to me when I was a little boy, "Son, the devil is crafty and second only to God in wisdom and power." But he is second—not equal!

"Resist the devil, and he will flee from you," says James 4:7. It is part of being spiritual to know the devil's ways. Paul said, "We are not ignorant of his devices" (2 Cor. 2:11, KJV). I do not mean we should concentrate on being experts regarding the devil. Those who spend their time trying to understand the devil more than they do getting to know God will inevitably fall like pancakes. And yet we should know Satan's ways and therefore realize how he plays into our hurts and jealousies, our weaknesses, and our pride. That is why we love gossip—the fodder for grieving the Holy Spirit.

DRINKING DEADLY POISON

Because the tongue is poison, we drink this deadly poison when the tongue is uncontrolled. We take poison into our beings when we say or repeat unkind things *about* people, when we say things *to* people that make them feel inferior, when we are not gracious, and when we speak out of fear. So if you and I do these things, we are not only spreading poison, but we are also drinking it. It is almost like committing spiritual suicide. Poison will either kill you or make you deathly ill. Speaking without thinking is tantamount to swallowing deadly poison.

Poisoned by what we say to others

How do we poison others? First, by what we say without graciousness to people directly. It does not matter how old they are or how young; how educated or uneducated; how cultured or uncultured; whether they are saved or lost; whether their ethnic background is red, yellow, black, or white. As Mark Twain said, "Kindness is the language which the deaf can hear and the blind can see."

Never assume that people will react to what you say with indifference. You may speak curtly to them and think they are thick-skinned and won't mind it. You are almost certainly wrong. People who appear to be thick-skinned happen to be among the most sensitive and emotional people of all. They cry inside but would never show it to you. What is more, when you hurt people, you grieve the Holy Spirit. And never assume a person is so full of grace that they can cope with your harsh words. Even Jesus was affected by what people said; He simply could handle it without sinning (Heb. 4:15).

When we speak without thinking to others, we may put temptation in their way and possibly even lead them to sin. Your words could speak fear into them. You could destroy them. This is why James calls the tongue deadly poison.

Poisoned by what we say about others

Secondly, we poison others by what we say to them about others. We could easily damage the person we are talking to; they may be crushed by what they hear from us. They may have a very high opinion of someone. They may hold a leader in high esteem. They may deeply respect another Christian. When they hear from us that so-and-so is not perfect (or whatever), it could wound the spirit of the person we tell this to. They may never get over it. In the process we may destroy another's reputation. We thus grieve the Holy Spirit.

What you say about others will almost certainly not be forgotten. You are responsible for shaping that person's opinion of others. They may never be able to feel the same way about that person—and you have this matter on your hands for life.

Always assume that what you say will be quoted. If you don't want it repeated, don't say it—ever, to anybody. How will you feel if what you say about a person gets back to that same man or woman? When it is quoted, it will continue to have a detrimental effect. Once a person learns what you said, they may never recover. The tongue is poison. Don't be like the person who once said to me, "I promised I wouldn't repeat this, so listen carefully; I can only tell it once."

Keep in mind that James is speaking like this so that (1) we will see that God isn't going to tie down our tongues; (2) we will mourn for our sin and be ashamed for the hurts we have caused in the past—and repent; and (3) we will see how damaging our words are to others. Seeing these things and being convicted by the Holy Spirit are what will enable us—with His help—to get closer to tongue control.

PART FOUR

MOTIVATION TO CHANGE

Submit yourselves, then, to God. Resist the devil, and he will
flee from you. Come near to God and he will come near to
you....Humble yourselves before the Lord, and he will lift
you up.

—JAMES 4:7–8, 10

THE PURPOSE OF JAMES'S EPISTLE IS TO CHANGE
lives. It was written to Jewish Christians, probably in Jerusalem
and possibly well before A.D. 50. It could be the earliest epistle in
the New Testament. The early Christians of Jerusalem needed to
be jolted. They had begun taking themselves too seriously, for-
getting the poor, and wanting to appeal to the more prestigious
Jews. (See James 2.) Their lack of tongue control caused serious
divisions in this early church. But it could not be more relevant
for us in the twenty-first century.

How do you motivate people to change, especially when perfection should be our aim and yet knowing at the same time it is
not an achievable goal?

I am a perfectionist. I have been this as far back as I can
remember. I was driven by a strong father who wanted me to
achieve. Making Bs in school when I was young was not good

enough. I was urged to make As, not even A-minuses! My church background, teaching "Christian perfection" as the church leaders did, only added to my problem. I realize that many readers may not have this problem, but I thought it might be helpful to some and also enable you to see where I am coming from.

My own dilemma therefore has been this. When I set a goal for myself, I want to feel it is reachable and that I can and will accomplish it. If it is an unrealistic goal, I tend to give up from the start. So when I know that perfect tongue control is not going to be realized by me while I am on this planet, I tend to say, "What's the use?" Therefore it has been a major step forward for me to set out to achieve what is not achievable, namely, controlling the tongue and never stumbling by my senseless comments.

So why have I made this step? Two reasons: First, I have been boxed in by my loving heavenly Father. I have made so many embarrassing mistakes that God has, as it were, put a pistol to my head to *change my manner of conversation.* It is as though the Lord has said, "RT, either change—or else." Second, our ultimate goal in life should be to please God. I hope I don't sound pious in saying that, but that's the way it is. We should have a desire that goes from the crown of our heads to the soles of our feet and to our fingertips to please God. God, by His grace, wants us to be like that. It is His grace that will give us that. Therefore we should want to pursue control of the tongue while accepting that we will only make measured, or limited, progress. But knowing that this pursuit truly pleases God is good enough for me!

I have prayed hard about this book. I have prayed hard to write in a manner that will help motivate the reader to want to change as we move closer to the conclusion of the book.

Chapter Eighteen

SCANDALOUS WORSHIP

With the same tongue we praise our Lord and Father, and with it we curse men.... Out of the same mouth come praise and cursing.

—JAMES 3:9–10

GOD INHABITS THE PRAISES OF HIS PEOPLE (Ps. 22:3, KJV). The more we see this, the more we will want to worship God, whether it be in private devotional time or in public worship with lots of singing. Our worship honors God and also brings about blessing to us for doing it. (See Psalm 67:5–6.) I would say this is true even if our worship is partly in the flesh, partly in the Spirit.

No worship here below will be perfect. Even on Palm Sunday when the multitudes of the people were shouting "Hosanna!" we learn that their worship was very selfishly motivated. But Jesus affirmed it all, knowing full well that they were thinking one thing (Jesus was going to overthrow Rome) and He was thinking something else (that He would go to the cross). Praising God for the wrong reasons is still mercifully accepted by God. And yet we wish for "a thousand tongues to sing my great Redeemer's praise," as Charles Wesley put it.[1]

IMPERFECTION IN WORSHIP

There are levels of imperfection in worship, and what James talks about here really gets close to the bone. When he speaks of praising God and cursing men in the same breath, I think of the following:

1. Going to church when you have been saying uncomplimentary things about that same church or its leader

2. Worshiping God when you are angry they are not singing a song or hymn you know—or like

3. Reading your Bible and trying to pray when you are in the middle of an argument with your spouse

4. Holding a grudge toward your enemy and feeling no shame as you are singing the praises of God

5. Speaking in an unflattering way about the same people who sit near you in worship

6. Singing hymns while feeling jealous about the accomplishments of a person who sits next to you

7. Praying and looking at your watch as you contemplate how you need to get away

8. Listening to the sermon and thinking about how someone else there is the one who really needs this

9. Asking God to bless you through the Word when you are preoccupied with those you have spoken against

10. Entering the service with anger from a conversation that just took place—and which is unfinished—and thinking of what you will say all through the service rather than worshiping and listening to God

11. Sitting in church—or at home in your quiet time— feeling no shame over how you have been entering into gossip

12. Expressing your love to God when you in fact speak ill of some who are His children and your brothers and sisters

13. Meditating upon God's Word without any sense of shame when you have just vehemently pointed the finger at someone

14. Praying for the poor of this world when you avoid them when the service is over

15. Thanking God for the blood of Jesus washing away your guilt while you have been an expert in sending people on guilt trips

The list could be endless. I came up with many of the above examples because they describe me more often than I dare think about.

James says that "this should not be" (James 3:10). True. No doubt. But that is the way it is. But if you and I aspire to a greater measure of the Holy Spirit and want to experience the "wisdom that comes from heaven," there needs to be some major changes in our lives. We begin with the tongue.

THE SENSITIVITY OF THE SPIRIT

A young preacher asked me recently if I had any advice for him. I replied, "Find out what grieves the Holy Spirit and don't do that."

The teaching that I have developed over the years that has been the greatest motivating force to improve in my personal life is the matter of grieving the Holy Spirit. I have dealt with this in considerable detail in my book *The Sensitivity of the Spirit*.[2] Here are some things I have learned about the Third Person of the Godhead:

1. The Holy Spirit is a very sensitive person. I don't really think it is possible to exaggerate how easy it is to grieve

the Holy Spirit. "Do not grieve the Holy Spirit of God, with whom you were sealed for the day of redemption" (Eph. 4:30). The word translated "grieve" means to get your feelings hurt. Like it or not, the Holy Spirit is a highly sensitive person who gets His feelings hurt—very easily. Like a dove, a very shy bird that cannot bear noise and tension, the Holy Spirit lifts and flies away when we grieve him. This leaves us to ourselves, usually irritable and unable to think clearly, having forfeited presence of mind.

2. We almost never know it at the exact moment when we actually grieve the Spirit. The departing Dove does not bring down thunder and lightning, He just unobtrusively flutters away—and we find later we grieved Him. Like Samson who did not know the Lord departed from him (Judg. 16:20), so we carry on as if nothing happened.

3. The chief way we grieve the Spirit is by bitterness. "Get rid of all bitterness, rage and anger, brawling and slander, along with every form of malice" (Eph. 4:31). We betray our bitterness by the way we speak to people and about people.

4. The Holy Spirit is no respecter of persons and will not bend the rules for any of us—whether we are church leaders with high profiles, veteran Christians,

or deacons, or whether we pray two hours a day or are counted as worthy saints by all believers. Those who enter into conversation that Jesus would not enter into grieve the Spirit.

GRIEVOUS GOSSIP

This brings up that ugly word *gossip*. I hate the word. It is what sells millions of cheap and tawdry magazines that are in your face as you check out of a supermarket. I so despise them that I like to think I am above this stuff.

I may not read these magazines, but I am just as guilty as those who do read them when I myself hear with glee that a person I don't like has been found out—and I pass it on. Or I repeat news of something unflattering about an enemy or a person who has wanted to hurt me in some way. Or I make a person feel good that I know would relish news of their enemy's difficulty. When I enter into conversations like this, *I grieve the Holy Spirit.*

Gossip is a defense mechanism to preserve our self-esteem. It arises out of an inferiority complex; we build ourselves up by tearing others down—or enjoying hearing that they are in trouble of some kind. It is a poisonous habit that betrays our insecurity and lack of spirituality. If gossip makes us feel better, we are self-deceived.

We may claim to be Spirit-filled, sound in our theology, faithful in our commitment to the church, zealous in worship, and have devotional lives that are highly admirable. But when we grieve the Spirit by bitterness, expressions that expose our envy and jealousy, saying what comes to mind that is not honoring to God, we become the very examples James laments: we praise the Lord and curse men.

He asks, "Can both fresh water and salt water flow from the same spring?" (James 3:11). If the well in us—the Holy Spirit (John 7:38–39)—overflows, one expects the fruit of the Spirit, such as love, joy, peace, patience, and so forth (Gal. 5:22–23). But when the Spirit begins to speak and suddenly there emerges harshness, anger, vengeance, and envy, something has gone terribly wrong.

This can happen when one preaches—apparently under the anointing—and then throws in a personal word that is aimed at someone in the congregation that the speaker thinks needs to be sorted out. It can happen when one prays aloud and then goes to moralizing others in the same prayer. It is when one lays hands on people to be blessed but speaks out against those who may not agree with the practice. Worst of all, it does not appear in the slightest to bother those who do this.

We have noted that the gifts are without repentance and are irrevocable (Rom. 11:29). Strange as it may seem, a person's gift may continue to flourish while the Dove flies away! This is because you don't necessarily need the fruit of the Spirit for the gifts to function. Grieving the Spirit pertains more to the fruit—love, joy, peace—than to the gifts of the Spirit.

What motivates me to improve is that I do not want to grieve the Holy Spirit—not because I fear I will lose my salvation or my gift; I am so afraid of losing the anointing. I know exactly what

Billy Graham meant when he said that his greatest fear is that God would take His hand off him.

The Holy Spirit will not produce gossip, hate, anger, revenge, envy, sensuality, lust, or selfish ambition any more than a fig tree can bear an olive or a grapevine bear a fig (James 3:12–16). It is impossible for the Holy Spirit to produce other than the fruit, such as love, joy, peace, and self-control.

REVIVAL FOR THE TONGUE

It is scandalous—offensive to God, and should be to all of us—when we worship and praise Him, sit under the teaching of the Word, and enjoy the fellowship of believers when we threaten the unity of the Spirit by words that reveal bitter hearts. I pray for revival. I sometimes think that revival will come when we, like those described in the early chapters of Acts, are together and have such a care for one another that we are detached from earthly and material concerns. (See Acts 2:44–45; 4:32.) This had obviously subsided by the time James wrote his epistle. I am not calling for people to sell all they own and give it away. I am only referring to the kind of care that once pervaded the early church.

Revival tends to make things that matter so much mean so little. For example, just before the Cane Ridge Revival in 1801, there were several denominations in Kentucky that were at each other's throats—largely over doctrine. A rival spirit prevailed with those who said, "Baptism is by immersion," "You cannot lose your salvation," "There should be no music in the church," "We are the true church," and things like that. Churches rejoiced when their rivals were low in attendance or when one crossed a theological line and joined them. But at the height of the Cane Ridge Revival (I have read the original accounts), *these things just did not matter!* There was such love and mutual acceptance that rivalries and differences evaporated—that is, until the revival subsided.

James knew who the real Holy Spirit is and what He is like. It grieved him to see a rival spirit emerge in the Jerusalem church. It should grieve all of us when we participate in scandalous worship rather than in the unity of the Spirit.

Chapter Nineteen

MEETING ANOTHER'S N-E-E-D

A man finds joy in giving an apt reply—and how good is a timely word!

—PROVERBS 15:23

AT WESTMINSTER CHAPEL I INTRODUCED A prayer covenant that over three hundred members promised to pray every day, and one of the petitions was that each of us would "speak only blessings into people's lives and to speak evil of no one." It was life changing for all of us. Those were wonderful, wonderful days. Hardly a week went by when, in the vestry before a service when the deacons met to pray, someone did not gently slap another's wrist with the phrase "Speak blessings!" when one expressed an annoyance over something. Often it was I who would be cautioned by one of them! The easiest thing in the world is to be negative, to say what you feel, to express being upset over someone's conduct, or to be critical.

172

That prayer covenant was born during one of our vacations in America when I heard our friend Randy Wall give a Bible study. He told how people can say a word in jest but be a little sarcastic and how it would leave a person feeling heavy for the rest of the day. I will never forget Randy's words: "I want to speak blessings into people's lives when I speak." He based the statement on two verses:

Let your conversation be always full of grace, seasoned with salt, so that you may know how to answer everyone.

—COLOSSIANS 4:6

Do not repay evil with evil or insult with insult, but *with blessing*, because to this you were called so that you may inherit a blessing.

—1 PETER 3:9, EMPHASIS ADDED

My sermon from these verses, called "Speaking Blessings," was for a while the most ordered tape in our library.

We all need to be reminded to be positive, not to be negative, and to speak words that will make another person feel—well, just *good*. "The tongue of the wise brings healing" (Prov. 12:18).

There are basically two kinds of people: energizers and drainers. Some people energize me! I love to be around people like that. They have a way of affirming you, dignifying you, making you feel esteemed and important, and leaving you with fresh energy. There are those who—sadly, even when you see them coming—give you a heavy feeling. You know they will be critical, say something that is negative, point out what is wrong, and leave you drained and in need of a rest!

What we should aim for, I believe, is to speak so as to meet another's *need*. Negative people will often say, "If I don't say it, nobody will," justifying their words. Of course, there are times when a word needs to be said—lovingly and gently—that is negative. A lot in this book is negative, as I had to point out wrong things certain people described in the Bible have said. Moreover, James is being negative when he calls the tongue "a fire" or "deadly poison." I pray, therefore, that this book will be emancipating for every reader.

So when *do* you speak negatively, and when do you say what is always positive? I answer: when it meets another person's true *need*. The best advice would be Jesus's words, often called the Golden Rule: "Do to others as you would have them do to you" (Luke 6:31). Therefore *say* unto others what you would have them say unto you. I have treasured words that were put to me, which could be construed as negative, as when Josif Tson said to me, "RT, you must totally forgive them"—a word that did not particularly bless me at the time (to put it mildly). But it set me free. That moment with Josif Tson turned out to be my finest hour. So a negative word, fitly spoken and well timed, can be a tremendous blessing. It sets one free.

But how do we know when we will have that precise effect upon another when we speak? I have come up with an acrostic that I have applied for a number of years. It has worked many times to energize people but also to keep me from saying what I could regret. I ask myself four questions before I speak to a person, all geared to do one thing—to meet their need:

N – Is it necessary?
E – Does it emancipate?
E – Does it energize?
D – Does it dignify?

- N -

The first question we need to put to ourselves is *whether it is necessary* to say something. I could have saved myself so much grief over the years had I put this question to myself before speaking: "Do I need to say this? Is it necessary that I say this?" If I were totally honest, I think that in most cases when my words backfired, it was because there was no need whatsoever for me to say what I said.

Every minister—in public or in private—should be controlled by this question: "Is it necessary to say what I am about to say?" When in the pulpit one should ask—whether it be a clever word, a joke, a humorous word, or even if it is theologically sound: "Is it really necessary to say this *now?*" I know what it is to be tempted to make a statement that, if I really said it, would mean I would very possibly lose the anointing that was with me up to that moment. I will say to myself, "But this will make them laugh," or "I see someone out there who needs this," or "Since this is good theology, it can't go wrong." I seek to justify what I am tempted to say when I know in my heart of hearts it is not necessary to say this now. I have to do some quick thinking—in a split second. Moreover, it may seem to be a hard call to make when you are speaking on your feet before a crowd. But I have learned that if it is not *necessary* to say it, I am better off to forfeit saying it. I seldom regret what I did not say; I often regret what I did say.

I never will forget one of the worst mistakes I ever made publicly at Westminster Chapel. It came early in my ministry there at a Communion service on Sunday evening. Only one week before, we had launched a campaign to raise a lot of money to redecorate the chapel and to repair the pipe organ. Being an American, I wanted success overnight. I anticipated a big response at once. But the British are different! I felt that the people were not responding to the appeal as they should have, and I sadly said so at the Communion table. I could hear peoples' sighs as I spoke. I knew immediately I had made a mistake. Mercifully we all got over it. I survived, and it was eventually forgotten. But my comment was *so* unnecessary. It taught me a lesson.

Most quarrels that Louise and I have had in our forty-seven years of marriage were unnecessary. They came from a little spark—such as, "Why did you do that?" "What did you mean by that?" "That comment was totally unnecessary" (which was probably an unnecessary thing to say). Our arguments could have been largely diffused, if not avoided, had we measured our response with the question: "Is it necessary that I say this?"

When you have to say something that is dealing with a negative situation, your words still will make the difference. For example, it may be necessary to approach a person who is involved in something wrong—and you are the only person who can do something about it. If so, what you say and how you say it can determine the entire outcome. Never forget Paul's words:

> Brothers, if someone is caught in a sin, you who are spiritual should restore him gently. But watch yourself, or you also may be tempted.
>
> —GALATIANS 6:1

The King James Version says that we should restore one "in the spirit of meekness." This means that you will speak in a manner that is not self-righteous. You will be saying to that person, "I could so easily have done what you have done—I am no different from you."

In other words, it was necessary to say something. But approaching the same person with the pointed finger in a condemning and harsh way would be totally counterproductive.

If we look back on words that we regret saying, it may be surprising how often you would have to admit, "I did not need to say that at all. I wish I had not said it."

This is what James means by being quick to listen, slow to speak, and therefore slow to become angry (James 1:19). If we are quick to listen, we will more likely have the presence of mind to ask ourselves, "Is it necessary that I say this?" After all, "a fool shows his annoyance at once" (Prov. 12:16).

This is not to imply that when one speaks when it is necessary that the words will always go down well. I recall standing up in a ministers' meeting with many important churchmen present.

I questioned a decision that was about to be taken. It changed my relationship with some present, but I have not regretted what I said.

Bottom line: if what you are about to say is not necessary, *don't say it!*

- E -

The second question I believe we should ask is, "Will what I say *emancipate*? Will my words set them free?" If it was necessary to say it, one may surmise that it will also set them free. Possibly. But we need all four questions of this acrostic to coalesce. I would say that if what I am about to say does not set a person free, it means it is not necessary to say it! I say that because, if it is not an emancipating word, it is probably not a necessary word in the first place. Jesus said that it is the truth that sets one free (John 8:32). But, as we will see below, the truth must be presented in such a way as to dignify the person. It is what Paul means by "speaking the truth in love" (Eph. 4:15).

When Paul said, "Let your gentleness be evident to all" (Phil. 4:5), he was addressing a fairly serious church squabble in Philippi. Two strong women in the church—Euodia and Syntyche—were apparently not speaking to each other. Each of them seemed to have a personal following, and a division emerged in the church. Paul pleaded with them "to agree with each other in the Lord" (v. 2). He then appealed for all in Philippi, simply, to be gentle; the KJV uses the word *moderation* (v. 5). The Greek word *epeiekes* comes from a root word that means "reasonable" or "not unduly rigorous." The idea in Hellenistic literature meant not to make a rigorous stand even though you are clearly in the right. It cuts across a legalistic spirit when one feels it is right to be inflexible for truth. I would translate this word *graciousness*.

"Try graciousness," says Paul. It is what sets people free. It means to overlook what might vindicate you and clear your name. You put your personal vindication in suspension in order to be gracious. There is nothing more emancipating for people than this.

I vividly recall when a person I knew well was very angry with me. I was certain that they were at fault. Looking back, I would still say they really were at fault. I was upset and angry with that person. My natural inclination was to register not merely disappointment but disgust with that person. I wanted him to feel guilty and ashamed. I wanted to speak in such a manner that I could say, "Gotcha!" Mind you, it would not have emancipated him, but I would have won the battle (and lost the war).

Here is what mercifully happened. I was given presence of mind. I remembered my own acrostic, N-E-E-D. I knew that the noblest thing was to emancipate this person. But I did not *want* to set him free—he didn't deserve it! But by the grace of God I did it. Here is what I said: "I don't blame you for feeling as you do. I am not sure I would have handled things as well as you have. You certainly have a right to feel that way." The person melted. The situation changed. Why? That person was set free from the guilt he was probably already experiencing, not to mention the guilt trip I was about to lay on him.

It is hard to set a person free when you are angry. That was my problem. I was also being very self-righteous. The Dove was barely hovering over me! I was perilously close to grieving the Spirit and missing the blessing. I can only say that God was gracious to me. It was so kind of Him to put my own acrostic before me in the nick of time. It also helped to encourage me to be more emancipating with my words with offended and offensive people thereafter.

I remember how someone set me free. I was angry with a particular person on the staff of a former church. I wanted to give him a piece of my mind. I also wanted other people to know what had happened. But a wise and sensible person came to me and pointed out this person's background—how deprived he was and how he was so much less fortunate than I. This friend pointed out how I would alienate this member of the staff if I said what was on my mind, how an offended brother is more unyielding than a fortified city (Prov. 18:19). I calmed down. I was set free. What this friend said to me was necessary and emancipating.

The greatest thing a preacher can do is to set people free. If one preaches under the anointing of the Spirit and doesn't mix his words with getting at somebody, the result will be that people are set free: "Where the Spirit of the Lord is, there is freedom" (2 Cor. 3:17). The ministry of the Word is to set captives free. Some are in bondage from jealousy, some are in sexual bondage, some are in legalistic bondage, and some are in bondage to pleasing people. An emancipating word from God gives inner liberty, a healing inside.

You have the power to do this! You do not need to be a public speaker or a church leader or a Christian with high profile to do this. You can do this with your closest friend, with those you work with, with strangers, or whenever unexpectedly you have an opportunity to give a timely word.

One should seek to do this, whether speaking to hundreds, thousands, or to one other person. Jesus did that. He set people free.

- E -

The next question I would suggest we ask ourselves is, "Will what I say *energize*? Will my words to them provide energy, vigor, and renewed ability to cope?"

When I was at Westminster Chapel, I always prayed for wisdom in the vestry as well as in the pulpit. It would give me enormous satisfaction when people would come in with a problem and leave feeling energized. I could not always do that, but I tried.

This may be the hardest thing of the four items to carry out. However, here is a promise: if you *try* to energize them, you will almost certainly do them no harm!

After all, part of tongue control is not to send a spark that will ignite a flame, not to utter poison that will make them sick. So when we are trying to energize, it is highly unlikely that the fire of hell will erupt.

And I can promise one more thing: if you ask yourself, "Will what I say *energize*?" you are not likely to regret what you say to anyone—even if you don't energize them! Try to energize them, therefore, and you will not offend. Neither will you likely make them defensive. You probably won't "stick your foot in it" or make a comment that will upset them.

The way you energize is twofold: (1) what you don't say, and (2) what you do say.

Here is advice one can safely apply when you want to energize a person (what you don't say):

1. Make sure you say nothing that smacks of pointing the finger. Don't criticize. Somerset Maugham said that when people ask for criticism, they really want praise! Most people you meet already have a fairly severe problem with guilt. The last thing they need is to feel you are accusing them of anything. Remember, the devil is the accuser! Don't be the devil!

2. Say nothing that will make them fearful or the slightest bit intimidated. Be careful that what you say is not threatening or that it doesn't give them a feeling of being inferior. Don't talk down to them. Most people have somewhat of an inferiority complex, so don't add to it!

3. Do not say anything that will play into their jealousy. Do not puff yourself. Don't name drop. Do not talk about your good news. It is easy to find someone who will weep with you; few will rejoice with you.

Here are things you can do that will help energize:

1. Let them save face. If you happen to know they have done something that is wrong, give them a way out. Dale Carnegie, in *How to Win Friends and Influence People*, says that if you let the other person save face, you can win a friend for life![1] Cover for them, and protect their self-esteem; don't draw attention to anything that already has them feeling guilty.

2. Think of something that will give them hope— something to look forward to. We all need something to look forward to. God made us that way; He understands that. If you can say something that is optimistic and cheerful, this is what most people want to hear.

3. Encourage them to talk about themselves. People love to talk about themselves. Let them speak freely about themselves. I learned from Alan Bell to ask people, "Tell me your greatest pain and your greatest pleasure at the moment." That will draw them out. When they feel you care, it gives them an energy they didn't have.

4. Ask them to let you pray with them—right there. If you sense this would make them uncomfortable, then tell them you will be praying for them. Ask them how you can pray for them—they will probably tell you. It sends a beautiful signal and gives a wonderful feeling.

Energizing another person is not the easiest thing to do. But do try. And, as I said, you will spare yourself from emitting deadly poison.

- D -

The fourth question you may put to yourself is, "Will I *dignify this person* by what I am about to say?" Dale Carnegie says that the greatest urge in the world is the desire to feel important.[2] We all want and need significance. When we treat a person with dignity, we will not start a forest fire! Forest fires by lack of tongue control come from demeaning a person, making them somehow feel second-class, insignificant, and unimportant.

I have long been intrigued that the common people heard Jesus gladly (Mark 12:37, KJV). Why? It is because they felt affirmed and important. He spoke in a manner by which they felt He understood them. He gave them dignity. Significance. Even a leper—utterly ostracized by society—knew he could get away with approaching Jesus, and he was accepted and cleansed (Matt. 8:2–3).

Here are some suggestions on how you might dignify a person:

1. Give them time. We show how much we esteem a person by how much time we give them. This is not always easy to do, especially if we are busy people. But if you want to affirm a person and make them feel significant, you must take time with them.

2. Look into their eyes. Even if they do not look into your eyes, look into their eyes. A person who cannot look into someone's eyes may have a problem with guilt or confidence. Make sure you look into their eyes. They will know they have your attention.

3. Smile. At least look pleasant! When we began the Pilot Light ministry in London (witnessing in the streets to passers-by), the hardest thing in the world for me to do was to smile. But I began doing it anyway! And what do you suppose happened? More people stopped to talk and would receive my pamphlet.

4. Pay them a sincere and true compliment—if it is not contrived. Don't be phony; they will see through that. But if you try, you can find something about them that your instinct tells you they are pleased about: "I've heard a lot about you" (if true). "You have a wonderful smile." "I love your accent."

5. Ask them if they will please pray for you—perhaps not then, but it affirms that you believe in them. They will feel important in your eyes. It is possible that few people ask them to pray for anyone, and if you ask them, it gives them a higher level of significance. What is more, if you are like me, you need all the prayer you can get!

Bottom line: if you want to excel in tongue control, speak in such a manner that meets a person's need. You will not only be spared of regrettable words, but you will also actually bless people!

Chapter Twenty

LAUGHING AT OURSELVES— WHEN WE FEAR WE'VE BLOWN IT

If we are out of our mind, it is for the sake of God; if we are in our right mind, it is for you.

—2 CORINTHIANS 5:13

I THINK I COULD WRITE A BOOK ON THIS VERSE. I could entitle it "Paul's Profoundest Throwaway Comment." It was not really a throwaway comment, of course. But this particular verse is stated in a manner that might give that impression! It is a verse not widely quoted, probably not even often understood. Here are six other translations:

Whether we be beside ourselves, it is to God: or whether we be sober, it is for your cause.

—KJV

Are we insane [to say such things about ourselves]? If so, it is to bring glory to God. And if we are in our right minds, it is for your benefit.

—TLB

If we are "mad" it is for God's glory; if we are perfectly sane it is for your benefit.

—PHILLIPS

If we seemed out of our senses, it was for God; but if we are being reasonable now, it is for your sake.

—JB

Are we really insane? It is for God's sake. Or are we sane? It is for your sake.

—GNB

If it seems that we are crazy, it is to bring glory to God. And if we are in our right minds, it is for your benefit.

—NLT

I don't remember every sermon I have preached (believe it or not). I am told that I preached approximately 3,500 sermons in my twenty-five years at Westminster Chapel. But there are rare occasions (exceedingly rare) I can remember a sermon. And my sermon on 2 Corinthians 5:13—called "Laughing at Ourselves"—was one of them. I was really chuffed when I came down from the pulpit that day. *Chuffed* is a British word that means "pleased." The American equivalent, I suppose, would be "tickled pink." Anyway, it was because I felt that I really did understand what Paul meant in these rather strange lines. What is more, seldom had I preached a word that seemed to do so much good in setting some people free! All of us have feared at one time or another that we really blew it *big time* by our foolish comments.

Why do I close my book with this verse? In a word, it is because God wants us to leave our mistakes to Him—and let Him sort us out. If we feel that what we said was really, really bad—don't worry! God isn't finished with us yet. And if, perchance, our words were quite appropriate after all (blessed thought!), then those to whom they were spoken will have to deal with them!

This closing chapter is designed to help us not to take ourselves so seriously. We have a gracious God.

"TO GOD WITH IT"

To grasp and fully appreciate this intriguing verse—2 Corinthians 5:13—we need to see the context of Paul's statement. Paul's relationship with the church at Corinth was very vulnerable at that time. Some evil people—usually called "Judaizers" (Jews who professed to be Christians who wanted to bring Gentiles under the Law)—went to Corinth to undermine Paul's ministry and influence. They largely succeeded, causing some of Paul's own converts to doubt his apostleship, authority, and authenticity. He took it hard. As F. F. Bruce put it, Paul sometimes wore his feelings on his sleeves.

The reason Paul wrote what he did in 2 Corinthians 5:13 is that he had just said something that his critics might seize upon and pick to pieces. He knew he would be seen as edging close to making himself look good when he said, "What we are is plain to God, and I hope it is also plain to your conscience" (2 Cor. 5:11). He realizes this is implying that all should see that his conscience is clear before God—therefore let all take notice!

But he admittedly said this looking over his shoulder at his critics. He insists he wasn't being defensive, but he was only saying what could make his supporters in Corinth justly proud of him—and have an answer to those who had been so critical. So here is our verse in context:

> What we are is plain to God, and I hope it is also plain to your conscience. We are not trying to commend ourselves to you again, but are giving you an opportunity to take pride in us, so that you can answer those who take pride in what is seen rather than in what is in the heart. If we are out of our mind, it is for the sake of God; if we are in our right mind, it is for you.
>
> —2 CORINTHIANS 5:11–13

Whereas Paul says, "We are not trying to commend ourselves to you again," the critics will retort, "You certainly *are* trying to commend yourself; you are clearly defending yourself. How stupid do you think we are? Methinks the man doth protest too much" (to recall Shakespeare's famous line).

In this book I have said that the greatest freedom is having nothing to prove. But critical people reading Paul's words will say that he obviously needs to prove himself by speaking of his conscience before God and man. He apparently thought this might make his loyal supporters feel all the better in their support of him.

But he also knows he has made himself exceedingly vulnerable. Should he have?

Paul might have taken these verses out before he let the epistle be sent. For he knew that some would say, "There he goes again, commending himself and trying to prove that he is a genuine apostle."

"No," Paul wants to say, "I am only doing this so that you who still believe in me can have a good reply to those who go by what is seen rather than what is in the heart."

Should Paul have said it?

One thing is for sure: he said it—and left it in.

But should he have taken these lines out before he sent the letter to the Corinthians?

Reader, what do *you* think? Do you believe Paul is commending himself? He says he really isn't trying to do that, that he is saying this for *them*. Do you think he is trying to win certain Corinthians back by showing how clear his conscience is before God? Is that not implicitly commending himself?

In any case, he thinks hard about it and decides to leave this verse in; then he adds, *"If we are out of our mind* [to talk like this], *it is for the sake of God; if we are in our right mind* [if I am, in fact, supposed to say what I said], *it is for you."*

He does not say whether he was right to say what he did. He just says, "*If* we are out of our mind ... *if* we are in our right mind ..." He leaves it open. We all can learn from this.

It is possible that the Judaizers had implied that Paul was mental. When a heated debate takes place, especially if one is losing the argument, some will accuse their opponent of being out of their mind—or mental. It's an old ploy. What we know is, Paul uses a word that can mean *insane*. The phrase "out of our mind" comes from the Greek word *existeemi*. It was said of Jesus in Mark 3:21 that He was "out of his mind," or "beside himself" (KJV).

Paul therefore says, "If we are out of our mind, it is for the sake of God." The Greek literally reads, "If we are out of our mind, *to God*." The translator threw in the words "for the sake of God." And the second part would be literally translated, "If we are in our right mind, *for you*."

It has to be said that what Paul declares smacks of borderline wisdom at best—and it is certainly debatable as to whether he was or was not commending himself but only helping the Corinthians. But the fact that he adds, "If I am out of my mind to say this," shows he is open to that very possibility, that is, that what he said was perhaps not wise. I am not saying his tongue was uncontrolled, for he was obviously in control of what he was saying—and had time to delete these words had he wanted to. I am saying, nonetheless, that he *may not have been wise* to make the claim that he was not commending himself by referring to his conscience before God. Paul knows that. That is precisely why he added, "If I am out of my mind"—that is, "If I should not have said this..."

Why, at the end of the day, did Paul say these words—and why are they important to us?

My answer is this: he makes himself an example of a person, like you and me, who has said something that is admittedly questionable—and what we can do about it afterwards. If we are able to learn from him, it will be a wonderfully emancipating experience for all of us.

Let us suppose, for the moment, that Paul was quite wrong to say what he did about his clear conscience. We have seen that he leaves open that possibility. What does *he* do, and what should *we* do when we fear we might have blown it? Paul himself simply commits it to God, as if to say, "Let God deal with me if I have blown it." And then adds, "If it turns out that I was right to say this—then you people will have to answer for it."

This verse—2 Corinthians 5:13—has upheld me more than you could ever imagine. Would you believe that I make a point to read it almost every day? I do! It is a most wonderful verse for those of us who realize that what we said, just maybe, was not right, that it was borderline activity, debatable conversation.

So what do I do when I wonder if what I said yesterday—or a year ago—was the right thing? I say, "To God with it!" Or as my friend Alan Bell suggested, "To heaven with it!" Yes! Leave it to God! If what I said is so horrible, He will sort me out. But if it should turn out that what I said yesterday—or a year ago—was quite in order after all, the onus is on those to whom I said it to receive it.

But the fact that I might not know for sure is not all bad; it will keep me from being self-righteous if indeed I was right! I might gloat. So God sometimes lets me remain in doubt—for my own good. This simply forces me to leave the whole matter (whether I was right or wrong) to Him. That will also keep me from the temptation to point the finger and say, "So there—I *was* right, wasn't I?"

There are some actions of the past in some of us that we will probably never, never, never know for sure whether they were right or wrong. That is, we will never know until we get to heaven. God also lets some things remain in suspension to keep us from taking ourselves too seriously!

And what is the best attitude to adopt from then on? I answer: we learn to laugh at ourselves. Leave it to God. Have a laugh! The truth is, God for the moment has chosen not to tell us whether what we said or did was right! We might as well laugh, because crying about it won't help! If you make a choice whether to laugh or cry, why punish yourself?

Giving something over to God is a great privilege. We cast our anxiety upon Him because He cares for us (1 Pet. 5:7). Once we cast our care on Him, leaving our burden with the Lord, we should not look back. The highest level of proof that we really have cast our care upon the Lord is to forget the whole thing and just laugh!

People who take themselves too seriously cannot laugh at themselves. They certainly cannot bear to be laughed at. But when we don't take ourselves too seriously, we will not take it so hard when we are laughed at; therefore, we can enjoy laughing with them—at ourselves!

What does Paul actually have in mind when he says "to God"? In other words, what is Paul counting on when he says "to God with it"?

Paul knows that God doesn't panic. He knows that God is big and powerful—not to mention magnanimous. Paul knows that God will eventually sort him out if he was wrong—and be gracious to the Corinthians as well. They too will survive. If the critics gain an upper hand for the moment, that too is OK. Perhaps Paul needs more humbling. Maybe Paul doesn't need to be seen as totally perfect in the eyes of his supporters all the time.

So why does Paul say "to God with it"? Because he knows full well that God will have a heart-to-heart talk with him eventually. God will put His big arms around Paul and say to him, "Paul, sorry about this, My son, but you really blew it." God is like that! By the way, God will do that with you and me, too. It may not be today or even tomorrow. But God has a way of teaching us a lesson—sometimes immediately, sometimes much later, as He did with Elijah (1 Kings 19:18).

God is in no hurry to give us the slap on the wrist or the shaking of the shoulders—or whatever we may need. I just know one thing: God tends to deal with me sooner or later, and often sooner—especially if it has to do with a cross word with Louise, my children, or a close friend. I am just thankful that He doesn't let me get away with things!

I have taken positions in my preaching—also stances on other matters—and I am still not completely sure what God thinks of these. I still hope He will tell me. I can think of dozens of occasions in which I said something, took a position or a stand, and received a lot of criticism—only to have God hide His face the whole time! I don't know if this means that my critics were right, if God was displeased—or what. I just know that He has hidden His face from me at times when I wanted *so much* to see His smile or feel His approval.

So what do I do when I look back on a sermon or public stance that I still am not sure about? I side with Paul: *if I was out of my mind, to God with it; if I was led by the Spirit, the people who heard it must answer for it.* In such situations I suspect I need not know for sure because, as I have said, I might take myself too seriously and gloat. So God leaves me alone, knowing I will survive.

One of the most controversial things I ever did was at a meeting of ministers several years ago when several of us watched a rather extraordinary video of Rodney Howard-Browne. Hundreds, if not thousands, of people in the video, listening to Rodney, were impacted by this ministry and were actually laughing their heads off! I never saw anything like it. I loved it, and they all knew it. But these very "sound," staid, and sober group of preachers in the room watching the same video were frowning, groaning, and, some of them, livid. While we watched this video, I whispered to the very grave preacher next to me, "You need that"—referring to the evident joy on the faces of those in the video. "Well, I do need something," he replied. But I made no friends that night with most of those ministers, especially when I scolded them for their closed minds and obvious recalcitrance.

Was I right to rebuke them? This, to me, was and still is a perfect 2 Corinthians 5:13 situation. What I said to them was borderline wisdom. It is debatable whether I was prudent. But as one translation puts it: "If we were 'mad' it is for God's glory; if we are perfectly sane it is for your benefit" (PHILLIPS).

I remember warning a minister who had vehemently opposed the things of the Holy Spirit. I was fairly sure it was because he did not want to risk losing his pulpit. He used to say, "If Tom Smith [not his real name] begins to accept this stuff, then I will say it is of God." Tom Smith within a year of that time did accept it, but this minister was still opposed. I reminded him of the conversation. He then brought in a different person: "If Harriet Reynolds [not her real name] ever accepts this, then I will say it is indeed of God." She did within a year, but he chose to stick to his guns. I warned him very strongly. A strain has been on our relationship ever since, although we remain friends.

Was I right to be so hard on him? That's another 2 Corinthians 5:13 matter. I sometimes wish I hadn't said anything at all to him; other times I think I was right to do so.

A lady used to come into the vestry after nearly every Sunday morning service at Westminster Chapel. She came in week after week with the same old problem. I knew what the solution was the first day she came in, but, remembering that "most people don't want their problems solved—they only want them understood," I patiently listened, nodded, prayed much the same prayer every time, and sent her on her way. But after about eighteen months of this, she came in after a service when (I think) I must have been in a bad mood. I can't be sure of that, but I know I decided to risk telling her what the real problem was. She never came back to the Chapel again. Was I right? I simply don't know.

Paul had a dilemma on his hands when so many people prophesied to him "not to go to Jerusalem." (See Acts 21.) He adamantly refused their prophetic words and got to Jerusalem as soon as he could. I take the view Paul should have obeyed the prophetic words, because Luke (writing under infallible inspiration) says that "through the Spirit" (v. 4) certain disciples urged him not to go to Jerusalem. This was confirmed by Philip's daughters and Agabus. Luke himself was clearly on the side of those who prophesied to Paul. Most people think Paul couldn't make a mistake like that.

The point is, rightly or wrongly, Paul went on to Jerusalem. Little apparent good (it seems to me), mostly trouble, followed. Fortunately the bulk of his work was accomplished by then in any case. But Paul alludes to this in his letter to the Philippians, because he knew they wanted to know how he was. His reply: "Now I want you to know, brothers, that what has happened to me has really served to advance the gospel" (Phil. 1:12). Fair enough. After all, all things work together for good to those who love God (Rom. 8:28).

This is the wonderful thing: "All things [do] work together for good to them that love God, to them who are the called according to his purpose" (Rom. 8:28, KJV). The fact that something works together for good, however, is no proof that what we did at the time was right! God is gracious and *makes* things work together for good. He did it for Paul. He will do it for you and me. We have such a gracious God. But we must never, never, never take the fact that something eventually turns out well as a sign we were right all along!

God does not want us to feel guilty. This is why we have Romans 8:28. As for the past, God says, "Leave it with Me." Once we turn over things to God, we can began to smile. And laugh. And let the past be *His* problem.

So do you fear that you have blown it by your faulty words? Leave it to God. Whatever you do, don't justify yourself. If you know that you were *clearly in the wrong*, I will now address this.

WHAT TO DO WHEN YOU ARE WRONG

What are we to do when we know for certain that we were in the wrong? Two things. First, confess it to God and pray that God will grant genuine repentance: "If we confess our sins, he is faithful and just and will forgive us our sins and purify us from all unrighteousness" (1 John 1:9). This is why Jesus Christ died on the cross. We must not try to atone for our sins by trying to put things right without looking to Jesus and His death. The only atonement that has value is the satisfaction Jesus's blood gave to God Himself. Trust His blood—plus nothing else. But do pray for true repentance—a definite change of mind—a further confirmation that you have been forgiven and that you can hear God's voice. This means you are not stone-deaf to the Holy Spirit. The confession to God, therefore, is not to be a perfunctory, glib acknowledgment of your failure and sin; it is with a heartfelt sorrow for your failure along with a sincere desire to please Him from now on.

There is, however, a second thing to do: do your best to put it right with the person you have hurt. Tell them you are sorry. If they don't feel like forgiving you, be patient with them and let them know you can understand their feelings. It is highly unlikely you will regret it when you try to put things right with those you have hurt. Can you do this?

James 3 was not given to us merely to make us feel guilty. James wrote these soul-searching words to change lives. Therefore when you see you have ignited the fire of hell or have spewed out poison to others, it is time to call a spade a spade and admit your sin to them as well as to God. Tell your heavenly Father and the one you hurt that you are very sorry indeed.

James's words are always a timely warning that we should make every effort possible to get it right when it comes to controlling the tongue. We are fools if you and I take his words lightly.

Conclusion

For by grace you have been saved through faith, and that not of yourselves; it is the gift of God, not of works, lest anyone should boast.

—EPHESIANS 2:8–9, NKJV

I BEGAN THIS BOOK BY SHARING MY MOST "unfavorite" verse in the Bible—Matthew 12:36, the words of Jesus: "I tell you that men will have to give an account on the day of judgment for every careless word they have spoken."

This is a very scary word from our Lord. Does it mean that every single word we have ever uttered—pre-conversion past, post-conversion past—will be played on a video for everybody to see and hear?

I answer yes, if we have not repented of such words. Being forgiven means not having them brought up to us again. When I forgive people, it is a commitment never to throw their wrongs up at them. It is over. It is forgotten. Not that I don't still remember them, but I make a decision never to mention it.

This is what forgiveness means—that God does not throw up what He has forgiven.

If you are saved, which means you know you will go to heaven when you die because your trust is in Jesus's blood and not your works, it is important that you walk in the light on your way to heaven. If a Christian falls into failure of controlling the tongue and does not repent, I would take the view that he or she will have to answer for that in the final day when they stand before God.

I close with these questions: Are you saved? Do you know for sure that if you were to die today, you would go to heaven? If you were to stand before God (and you will) and He were to ask you (and He might), "Why should I let you into My heaven?" what would you say?

Suppose that you wrote on a sheet of paper what you would say to God. It would be good if you took the time right now—before finishing this brief conclusion—to get paper and pen and write down in your own words how you would answer this question: Why should God let you into heaven?

Based upon fifty years of ministry, here are some of the most common answers I get to this question (and I have asked thousands of people—apart from preaching—in a one-to-one relationship):

1. I have tried to live a good life.
2. I have done my best.
3. I am a sincere person.
4. I am an honest person.
5. I believe in God.
6. I live by the Ten Commandments.

7. I have a lot of good works to prove that I have been a good person.

8. I have tried to be good to people.

9. I have been baptized.

10. I am a church member.

11. I have been confirmed.

12. I was brought up in a Christian home.

13. I give to the church and to charities.

14. I sent some missionaries some money.

15. I live by the Sermon on the Mount.

16. I believe in the teachings of Jesus.

17. I go to church.

18. I go to church at Christmas and Easter.

19. I sent money to Billy Graham.

20. I am a Baptist.

21. I am a Catholic.

22. I love God.

23. I have suffered a lot.

24. I believe in saying "Merry Christmas," not just "Happy Holidays."

25. I have been to the Holy Land—and had an awesome feeling.

If any or all of these possible answers would coincide with what you would honestly have written down, I must say lovingly but firmly to you that you are not saved and that you are not a Christian. This is because you are trusting in the good things you have done. The Bible says, "It is by grace you have been saved, through faith—and this not from yourselves, it is the gift of God—*not by works*, so that no one can boast" (Eph. 2:8–9, emphasis added).

Belief in God does not save. Even the devil believes in God—he is not an atheist (James 2:19)! Being a church member does not save you. Good works—the best of them—will not save you. Even if you have some success in controlling your tongue, this will not save you. Good works will even hurt if you think they will help you get to heaven.

The only way to be saved is to acknowledge that you are truly a sinner—that you have sinned before God and you are sorry for your sins. You must acknowledge that God sent His Son—Jesus Christ, the God-man—to live a perfect life for you and die for you. You must recognize that heaven is a gift of God—a gift that must be received before it is yours. You receive this gift by transferring your trust in your good works to what Jesus Christ did for you on the cross. You receive this gift by faith. Saving faith is more than calling on God when you are in need or in trouble. The faith that saves is when you put "all your eggs into one basket"—namely, the blood of Jesus. To help you, I would ask you to pray this prayer:

Lord Jesus Christ, I need You. I want You. I am sorry for my sins. I believe that You are the Son of God and that You died on the cross for my sins. I believe that You rose from the dead. I renounce hope in my good works. Wash my sins away by Your blood. I welcome Your Holy Spirit into my heart. As best as I know how, I give You my life. Amen.

If you prayed that prayer, share it with one other person. For here is the greatest thing you can ever do with your tongue: "If you *confess with your mouth*, 'Jesus is Lord,' and believe in your heart that God raised him from the dead, you will be saved" (Rom. 10:9, emphasis added). Begin to pray every day. Read the Bible every day. Find a church where the Bible is preached and Christ is honored, and get involved in that church. Grow in grace by walking in all the light God gives you (1 John 1:7). And remember that Jesus said, "I am with you always, to the very end of the age" (Matt. 28:20).

May the blessing of God Almighty—Father, Son, and Holy Spirit—be with you and abide with you now and forever more. Amen.

Notes

INTRODUCTION

1. "Amazing Grace" by John Newton. Public domain.

2. *John Newton of Olney and St. Mary Woolnoth: An Autobiography and Narrative*, compiled chiefly from his diary and other unpublished documents by Josiah Bull, MA (Carlisle, PA: The Banner of Truth Trust, 1998), http://www.cleavetogod.com/newton_chapter14.htm (accessed February 28, 2007).

3. Omar Khayyam, "The Rubaiyat," http://classics.mit.edu/khayyam/rubaiyat.html (accessed February 28, 2007).

CHAPTER 1
POINTING THE FINGER

1. R. T. Kendall, *In Pursuit of His Glory* (Lake Mary, FL: Charisma House, 2004).

CHAPTER 4
TRYING TO PROVE OURSELVES

1. *Hamlet*, 3.2. Reference provided by *The Tech*, online newspaper of Massachusetts Institute of Technology, "The Complete Works of William Shakespeare," http://www-tech.mit.edu/Shakespeare/hamlet/hamlet.3.2.html (accessed December 12, 2006). References are to act and scene.

2. *Much Ado About Nothing*, 3.5. Reference provided by *The Tech*, http://www-tech.mit.edu/Shakespeare/much_ado/much_ado.3.5.html (accessed December 12, 2006). References are to act and scene.

CHAPTER 8
CLIMBING DOWN

1. R. T. Kendall, *The Anointing: Yesterday, Today, Tomorrow* (Lake Mary, FL: Charisma House, 2003).

CHAPTER 9
IN THE PRESENCE OF AN ENEMY

1. R. T. Kendall, *Total Forgiveness* (Lake Mary, FL: Charisma House, 2002).

CHAPTER 12
THE TONGUE ON THE WAY TO CHURCH

1. R. T. Kendall, *Higher Ground* (Ross-shire, Scotland, UK: Christian Focus Publications, Ltd., 1995).

CHAPTER 13
ASKING FOR TROUBLE

1. George Bernard Shaw, "Maxims for Revolutionists," 36, in *Man and Superman*. Reference provided by Bartleby.com, http://www .bartleby.com/157/6.html (accessed March 1, 2007). Reference is to maxim number.

2. Laurence J. Peter, *The Peter Principle* (Cutchogue, NY: Buccaneer Books, 1993).

3. O. S. Hawkins, *Getting Down to Brass Tacks* (Neptune, NJ: Loizeaux Brothers, 1993), 93.

CHAPTER 14
THE PROOF OF SELF-CONTROL

1. Hawkins, *Getting Down to Brass Tacks*, 94.

CHAPTER 16
THE FIRE OF HELL

1. R. T. Kendall, *The Judgment Seat of Christ* (Ross-shire, Scotland, UK: Christian Focus Publications, Ltd., 2004).

2. "A Firm Foundation" by George Keith. Public domain.

CHAPTER 18
SCANDALOUS WORSHIP

1. "O for a Thousand Tongues to Sing" by Charles Wesley. Public domain.

2. R. T. Kendall, *The Sensitivity of the Spirit* (Lake Mary, FL: Charisma House, 2002).

CHAPTER 19
MEETING ANOTHER'S N-E-E-D

1. Dale Carnegie, *How to Win Friends and Influence People* (New York: Simon and Schuster, 1981).

2. Ibid.